PIANO · VOCAL · GUITAR

the twilight saga
breaking dawn
part 2

MUSIC FROM THE MOTION PICTURE SOUNDTRACK

ISBN 978-1-4803-2857-0

HAL•LEONARD®
CORPORATION

7777 W. BLUEMOUND RD. P.O. BOX 13819 MILWAUKEE, WI 53213

Visit Hal Leonard Online at
www.halleonard.com

WHERE I COME FROM

Words and Music by
MICHAEL ANGELAKOS

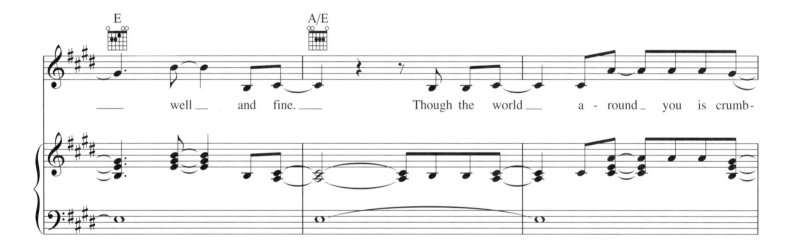

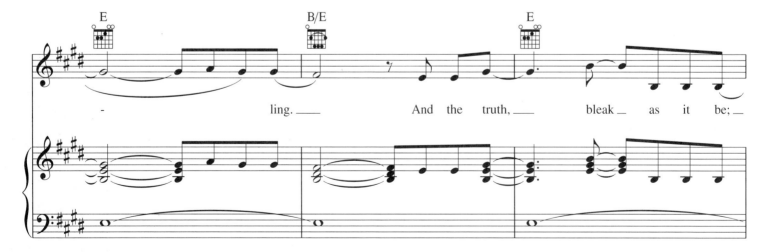

stay close, ___ be - lieve ___ that things ___ are not ___ what they seem. ___

I won't let ___ them de - stroy ___ these dreams _____ ap - pear -

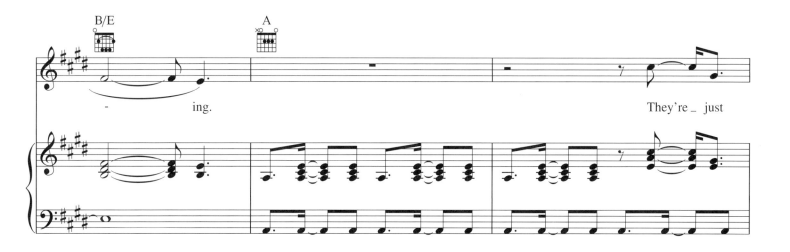

- ing.   They're _ just

things,   sil - ly lit - tle ___ things.

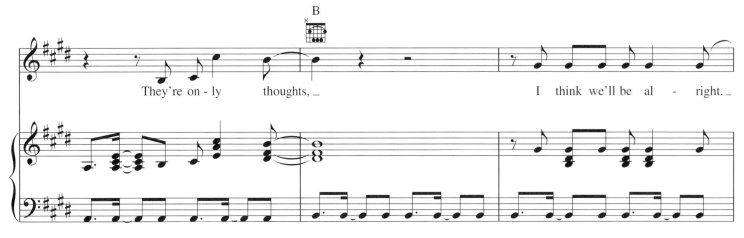

They're on - ly thoughts, _ I think we'll be al - right. _

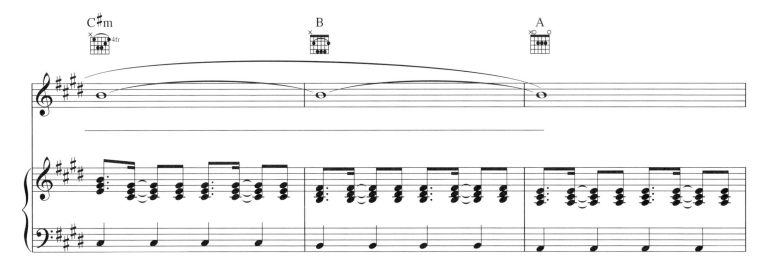

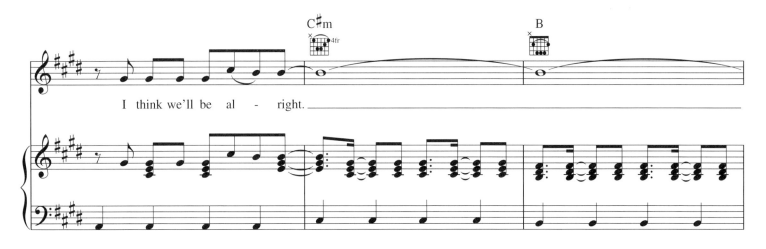

I think we'll be al - right. _____

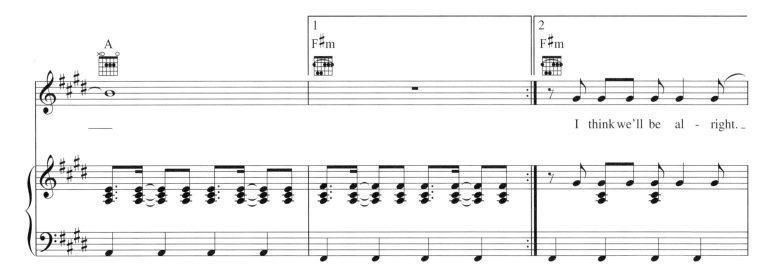

_ I think we'll be al - right. _

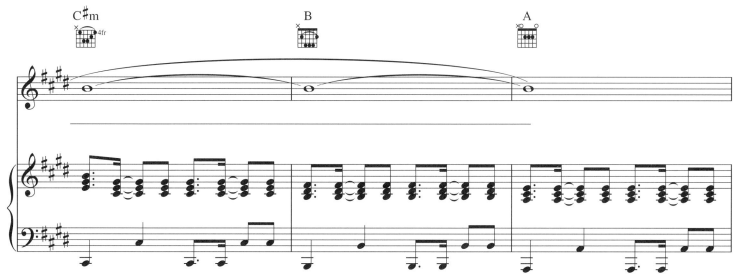

I think we'll be al - right. _____

Optional Ending

Repeat and Fade

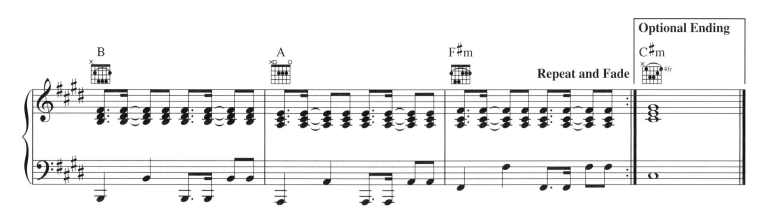

BITTERSWEET

Words and Music by SONNY MOORE
and ELLIE GOULDING

Moderately fast

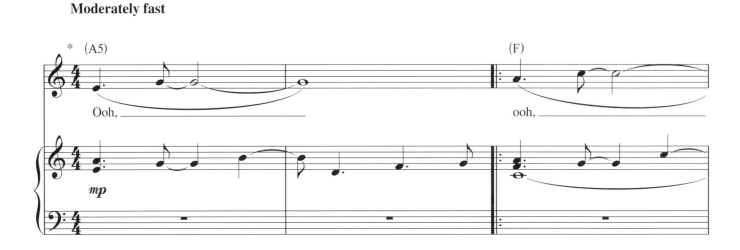

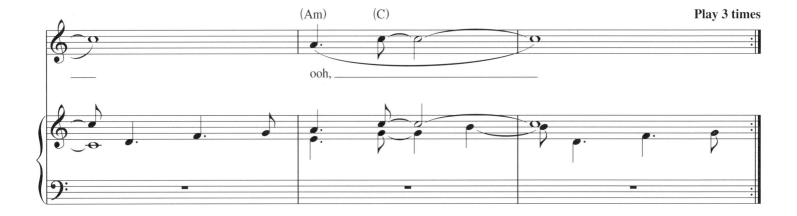

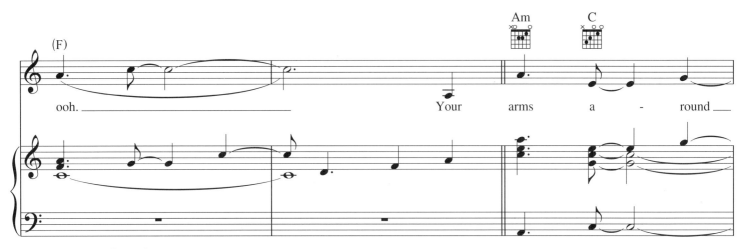

* Recorded a half step lower.

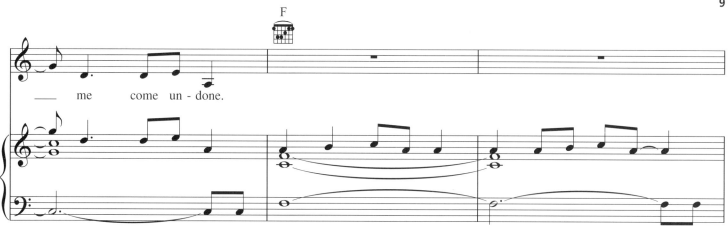

me come un - done.

Makes my ___ heart ___ beat like a drum.

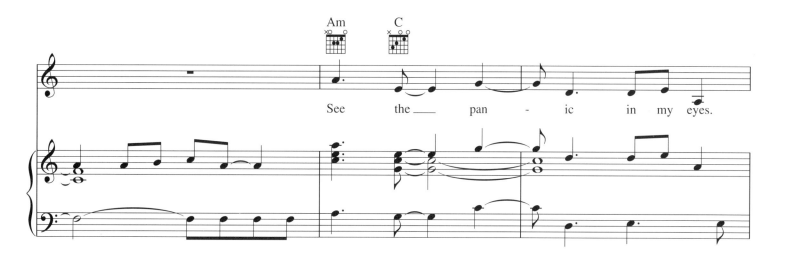

See the ___ pan - ic in my eyes.

Kiss me ___ on -

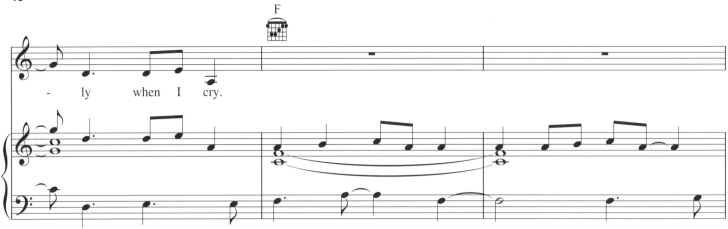

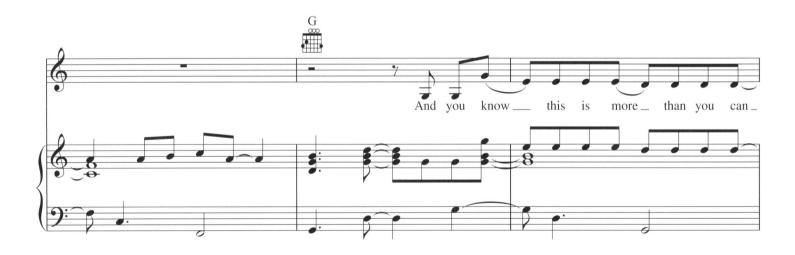

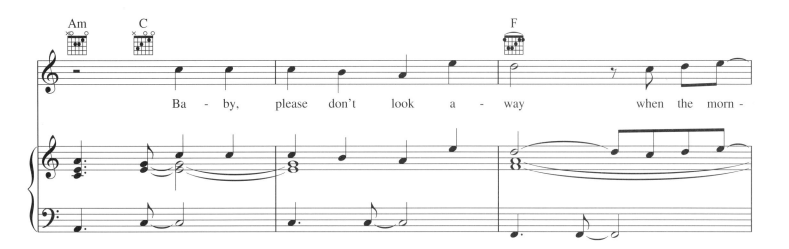

don't for - get my name _____ when the morn - ing breaks us. _____

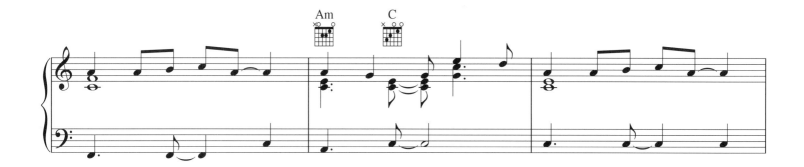

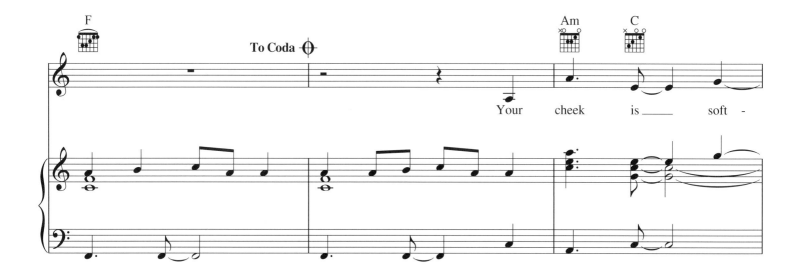

To Coda

Your cheek is _____ soft -

- ly by the sun, makes my — heart —

— beat like a drum. I know it hurts you.

I know it burns you. Hot and cold in a lone-ly ho-tel room.

Look in-to me, tell — me why you're cry - ing. I need — to know. —

'Cause you al - ways want _ what you're run -

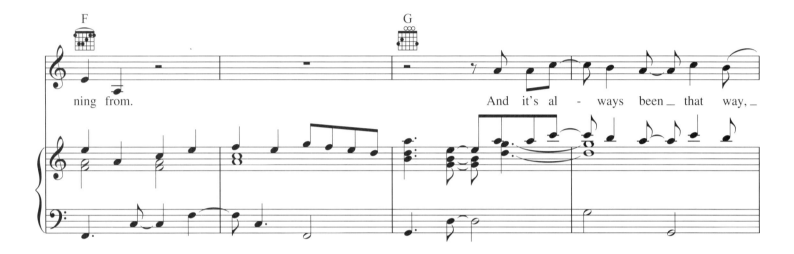

ning from.

And it's al - ways been _ that way, _

oh. _

D.S. al Coda

CODA

'Cause you al - ways want _ what you're run - ning from.

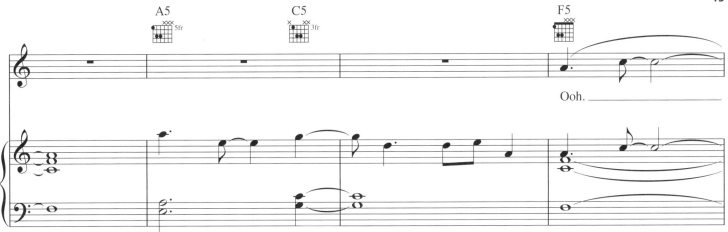

sweet, ahh. _____ Ba - by,

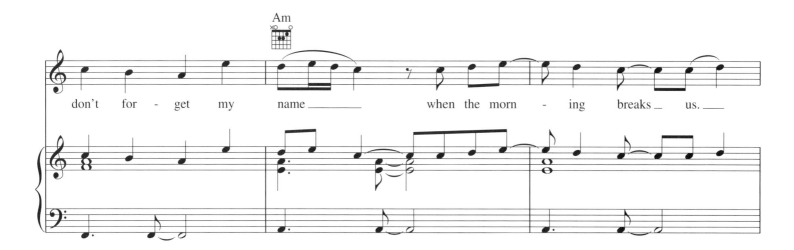

don't for - get my name _____ when the morn - ing breaks __ us. ___

Ooh, _____ ooh, _____

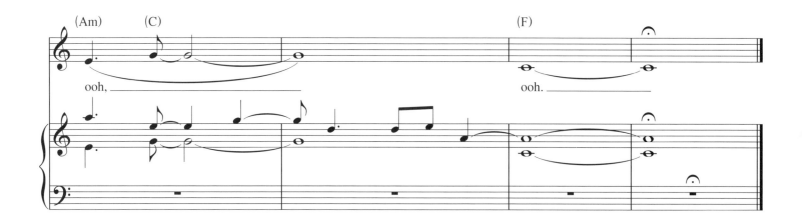

ooh, _____ ooh. _____

THE FORGOTTEN

Words and Music by BILLIE JOE ARMSTRONG,
MIKE DIRNT and TRE COOL

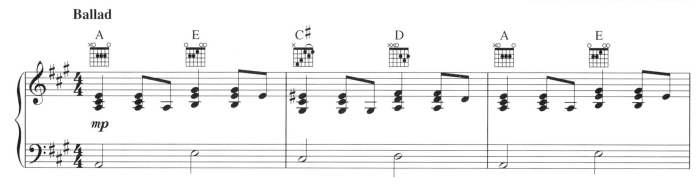

Where in the world's _____ the for-got -
Where in the world _____ did the time _

- ten? _____
_____ go? _____

They're lost in-side _____ your mem-o -
It's where your spir-it seems to _____

ry.
roam.

You're drag-ging on, _____ your heart's_ been bro -
Like los-ing faith_ to our_ a-ban -

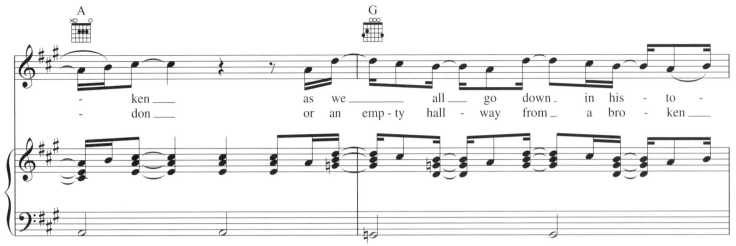

- ken ____ as we ____ all ____ go down ____ in his - to -
- don ____ or an emp - ty hall - way from ____ a bro - ken ____

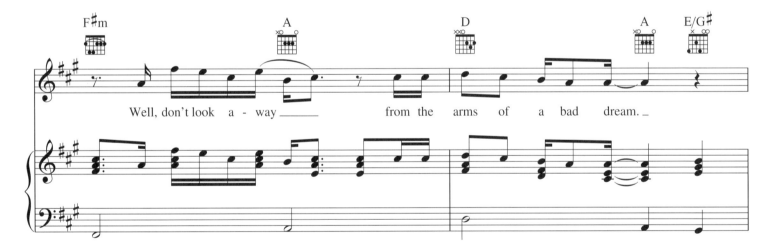

1
ry.

2
home.

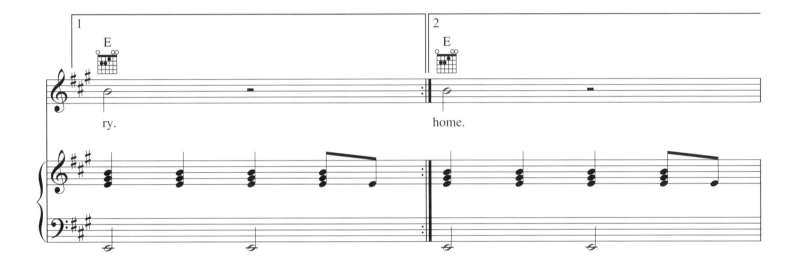

Well, don't look a - way ____ from the arms of a bad dream. ____

And don't look a - way, ____ some - times you're bet - ter lost ____ than to ____ be ____

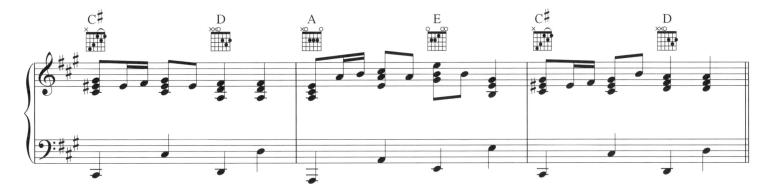

I don't feel strange, _ it's more _ like haunt - ed,
So where in the world's _ the ___ for - got - ten?

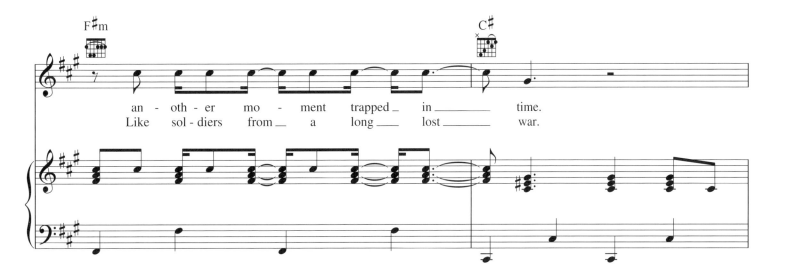

an - oth - er mo - ment trapped _ in ___ time.
Like sol - diers from _ a long ___ lost ___ war.

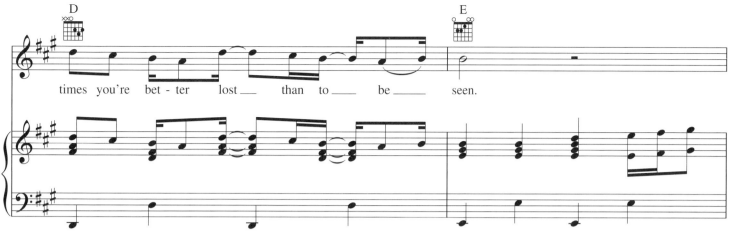

times you're bet - ter lost ___ than to ___ be ___ seen.

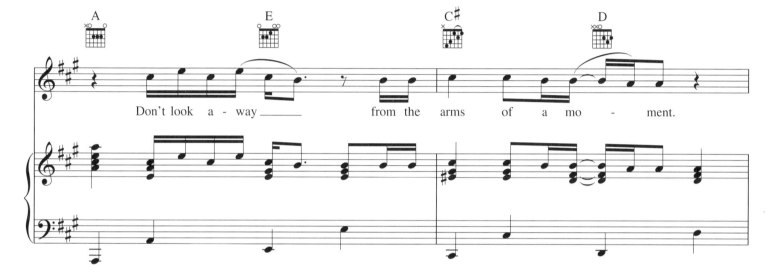

Don't look a - way ___ from the arms of a mo - ment.

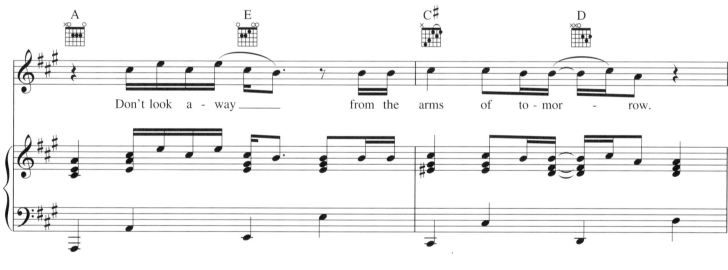

Don't look a - way ___ from the arms of to - mor - row.

To Coda

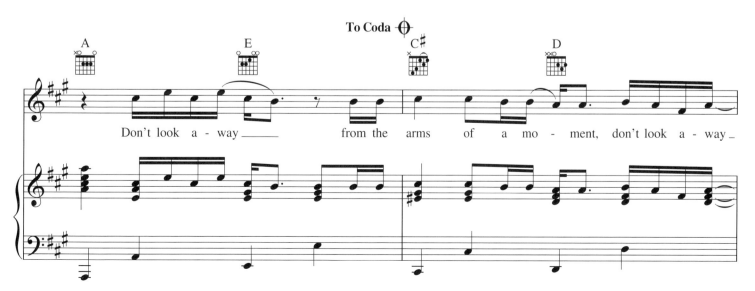

Don't look a - way ___ from the arms of a mo - ment, don't look a - way ___

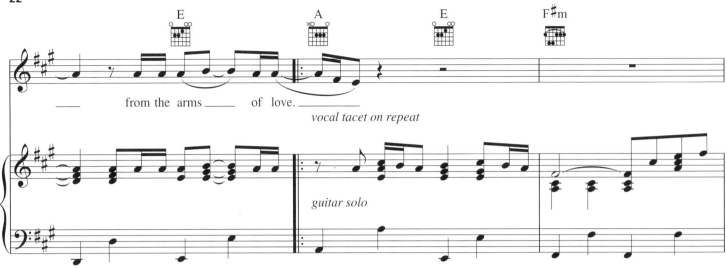

from the arms _____ of love. _____

vocal tacet on repeat

guitar solo

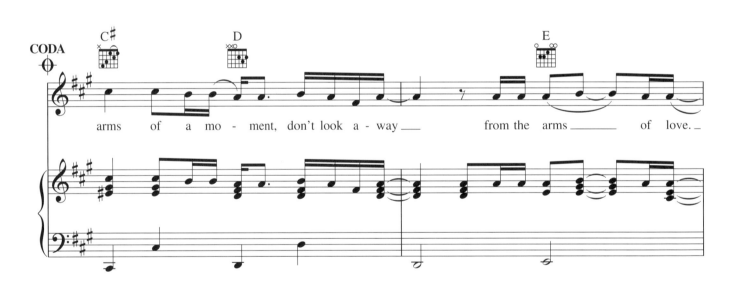

CODA

arms of a mo - ment, don't look a - way _____ from the arms _____ of love. _____

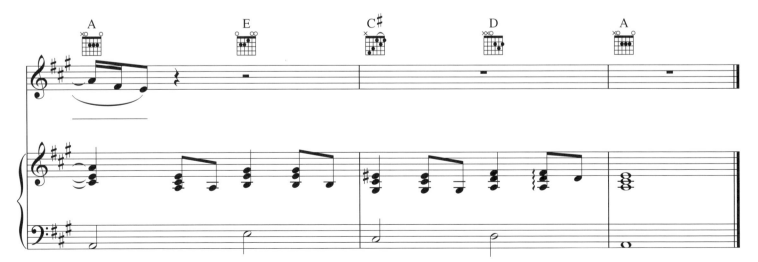

FIRE IN THE WATER

Words and Music by LESLIE FEIST
and BRIAN LEBARTON

Slowly, eerily

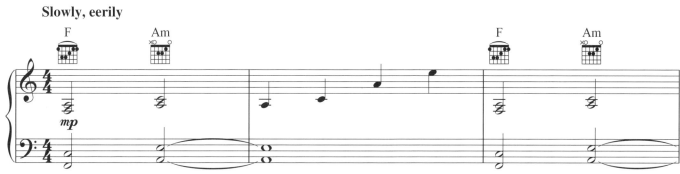

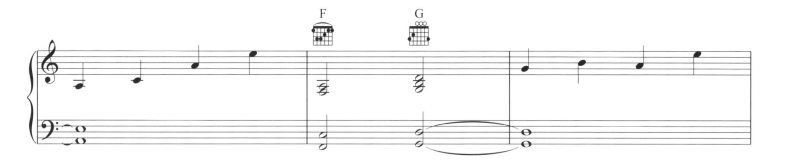

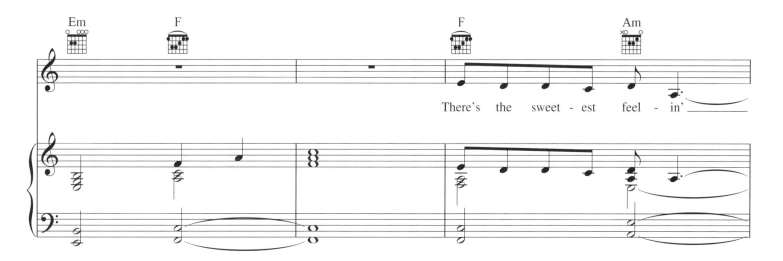

There's the sweet-est feel-in' _____ op-en-ly be-liev-in'. _____

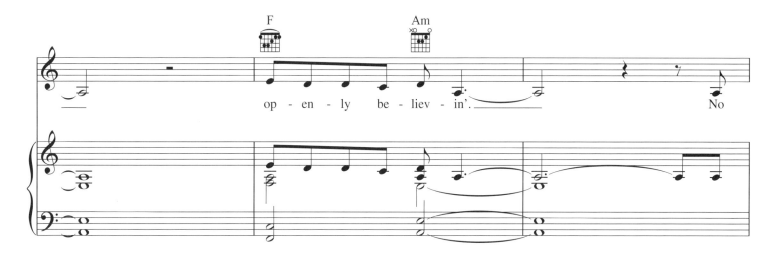

No

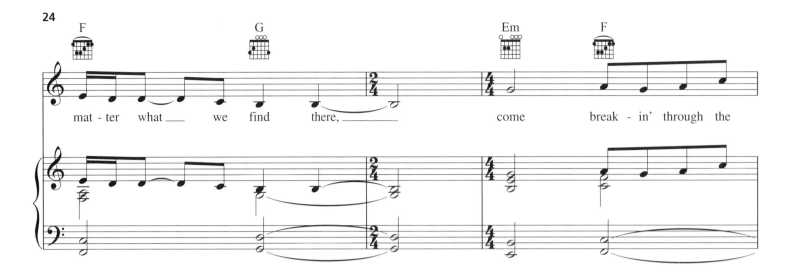

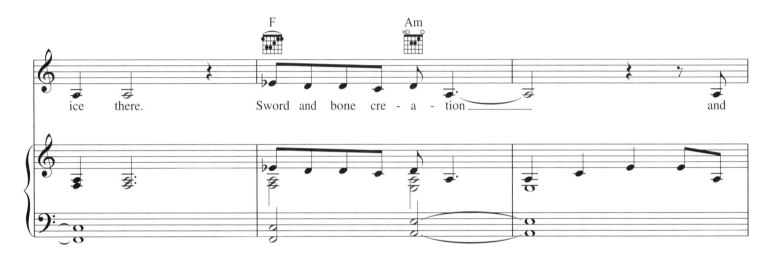

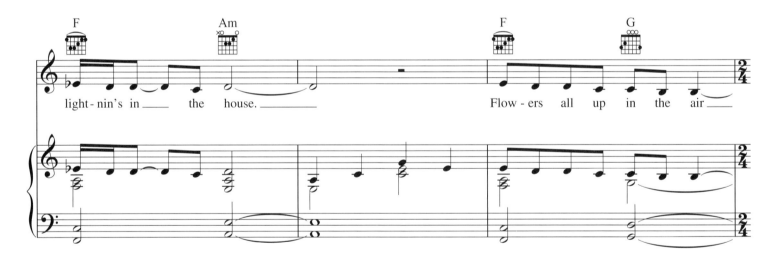

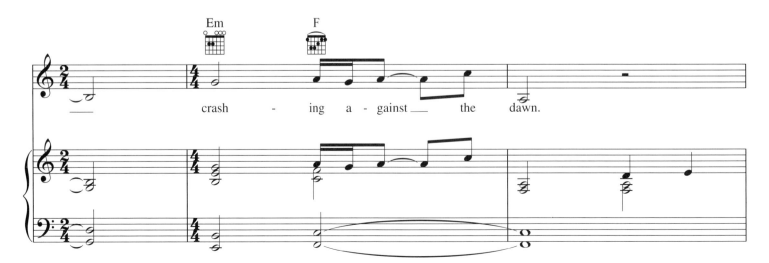

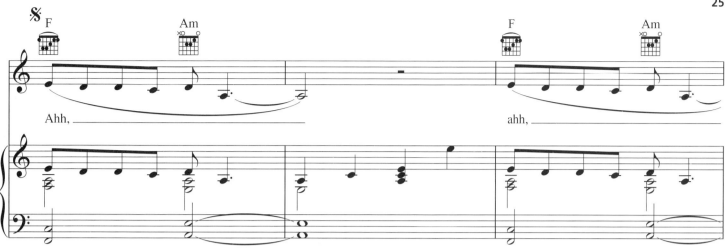

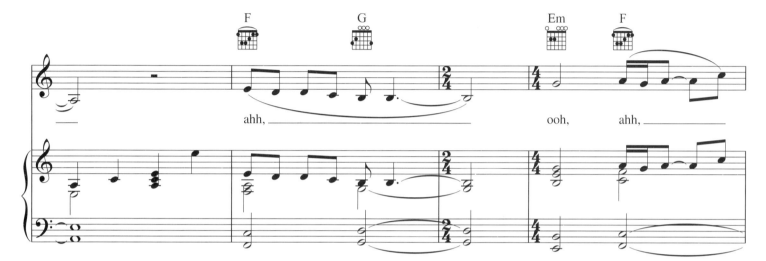

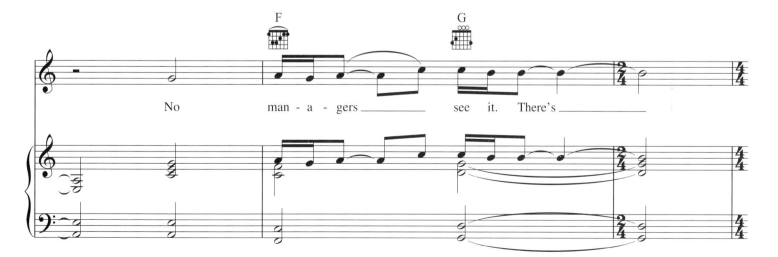

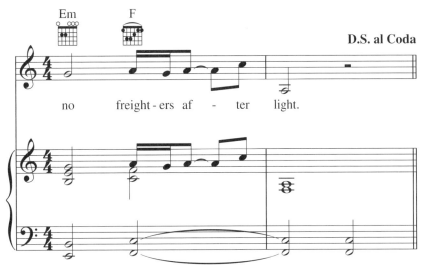

D.S. al Coda

no freight-ers af - ter light.

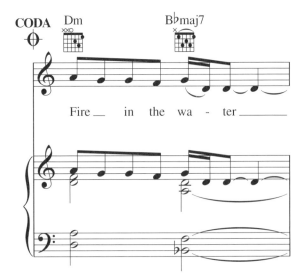

CODA Dm   B♭maj7

Fire __ in the wa - ter __

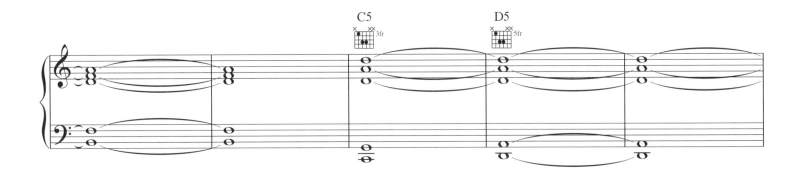

__ is the bod - y of __ our love, __ ooh. __

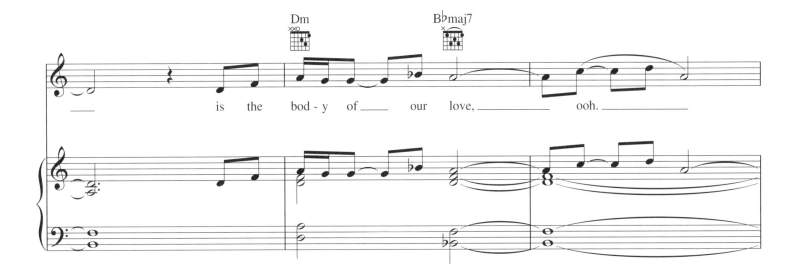

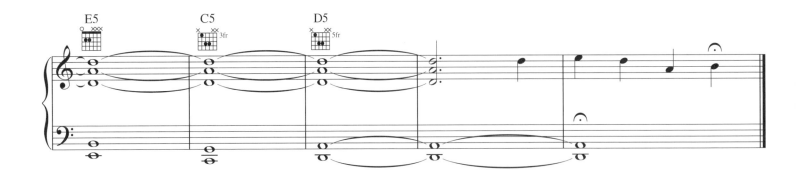

EVERYTHING AND NOTHING

Words and Music by ANDY ELLIS
and VEGA SCHENK

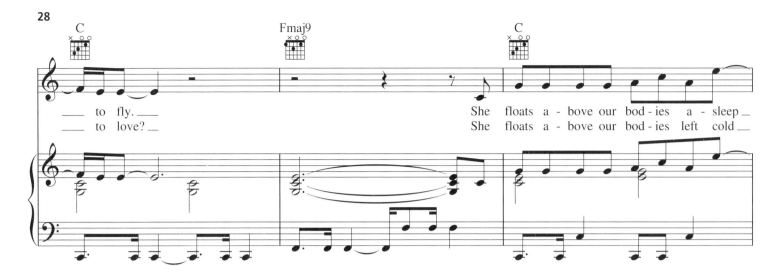

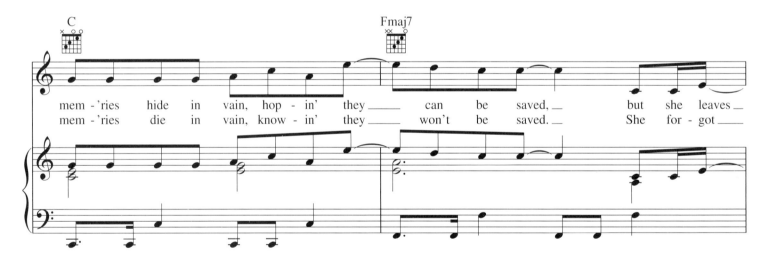

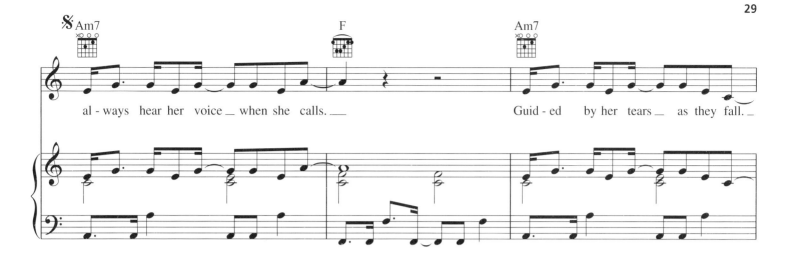

al - ways hear her voice __ when she calls. __ Guid - ed by her tears __ as they fall. __

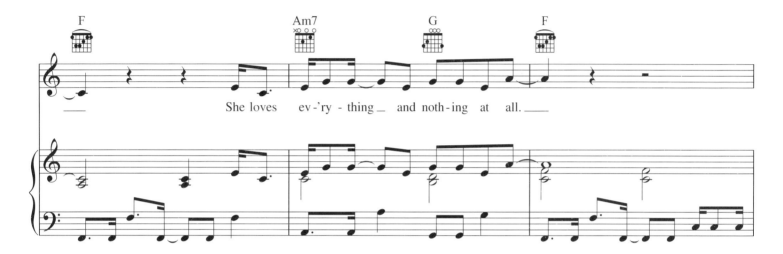

She loves ev -'ry - thing __ and noth - ing at all. __

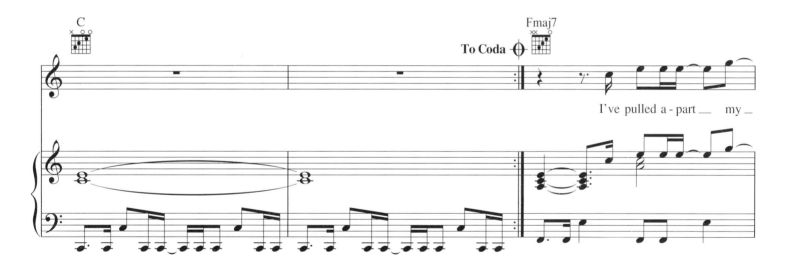

To Coda

I've pulled a - part __ my __

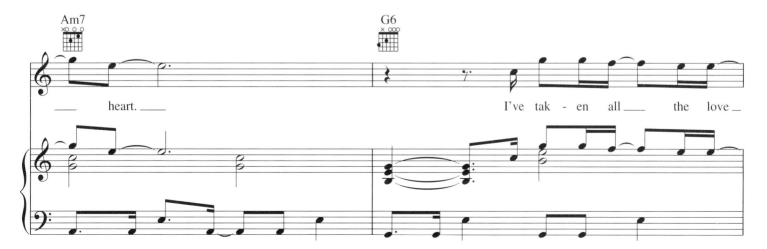

__ heart. __ I've tak - en all __ the love __

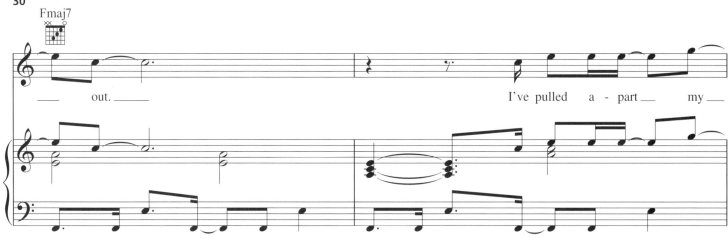

out. _____

I've pulled a-part_ my_

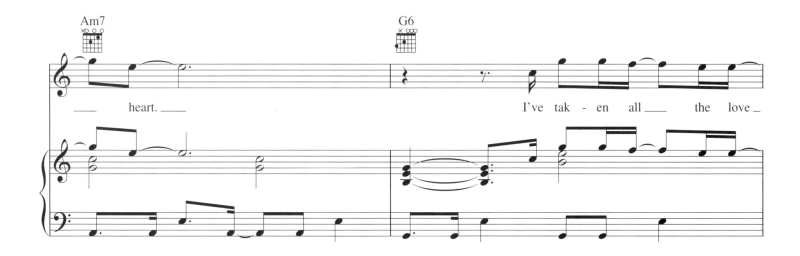

_____ heart. _____

I've tak - en all _____ the love _

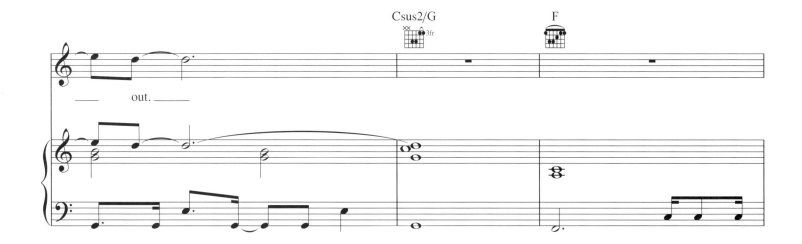

_____ out. _____

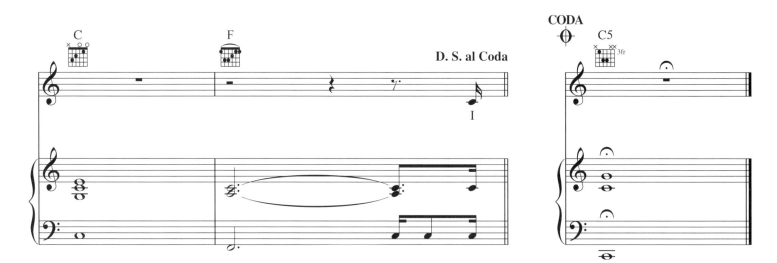

D. S. al Coda

I

CODA

THE ANTIDOTE

Words and Music by
ANNE CLARK

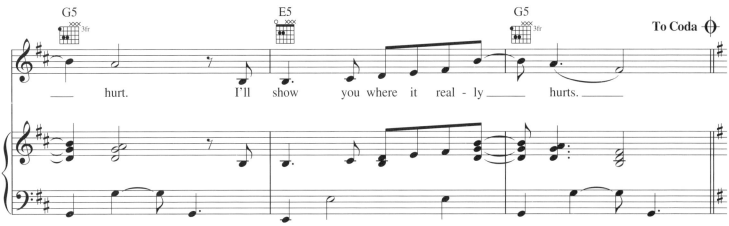

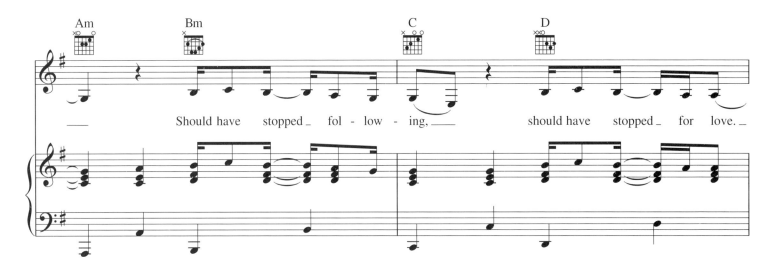

D.S. al Coda

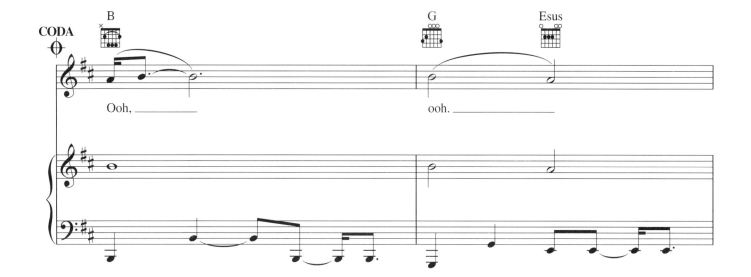

Ooh, _____ ooh. _____

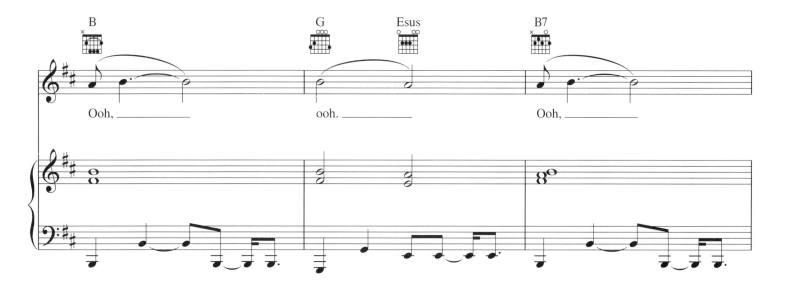

Ooh, _____ ooh. _____ Ooh, _____

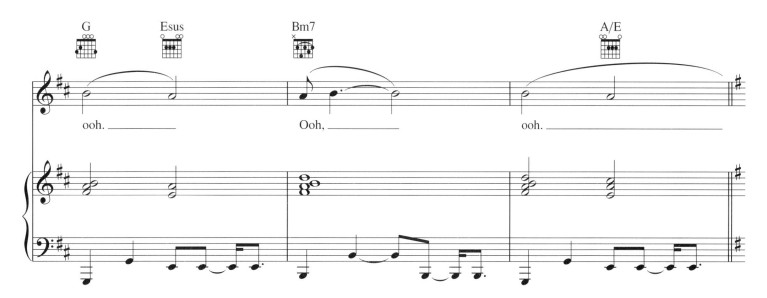

ooh. _____ Ooh, _____ ooh. _____

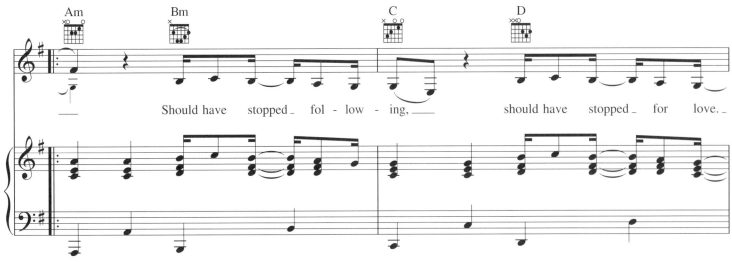

Should have stopped_ fol - low - ing, ___ should have stopped_ for love._

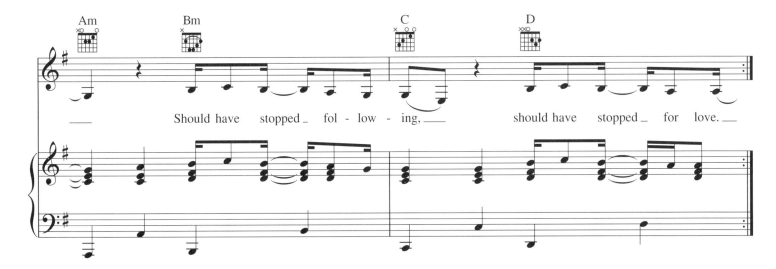

Should have stopped_ fol - low - ing, ___ should have stopped_ for love._

Should have stopped_ fol - low - ing, ___ should have stopped_ for love._

Should have stopped_ fol - low - ing, ___ should have stopped_ for love._

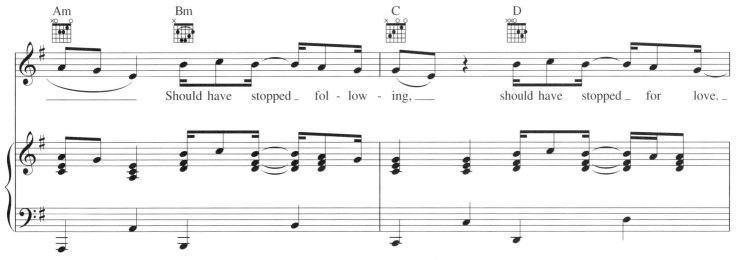

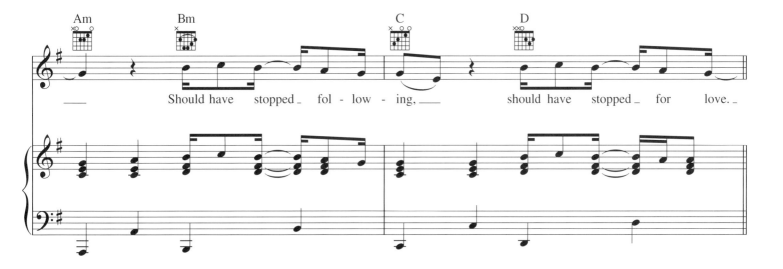

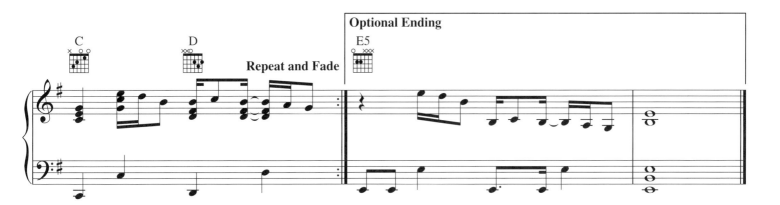

SPEAK UP

Words and Music by
CHRISTOPHER CHU

With movement

Play 3 times

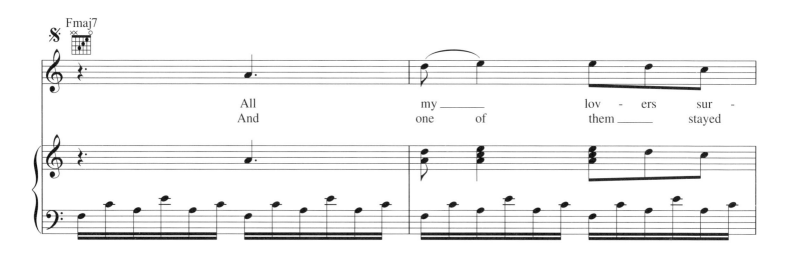

All my lov- ers sur-
And one of them stayed

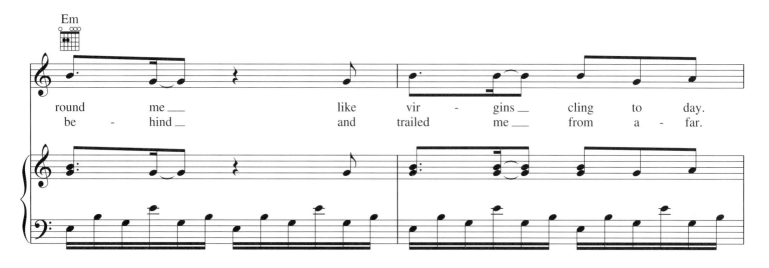

round me like vir- gins cling to day.
be- hind and trailed me from a- far.

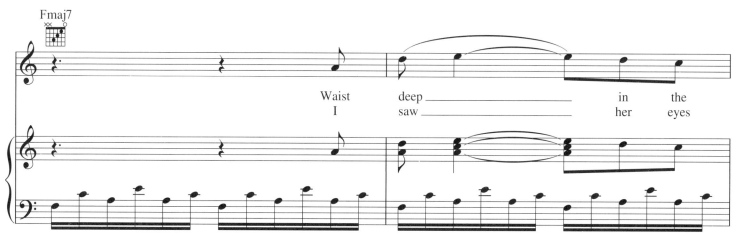

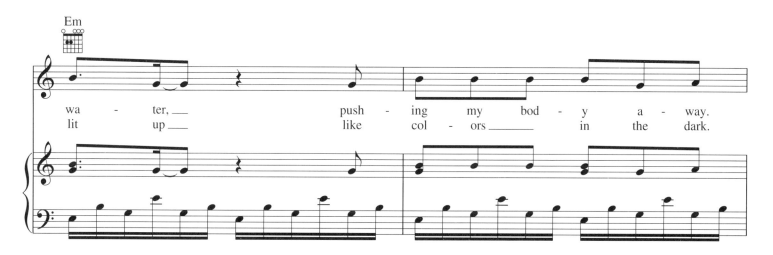

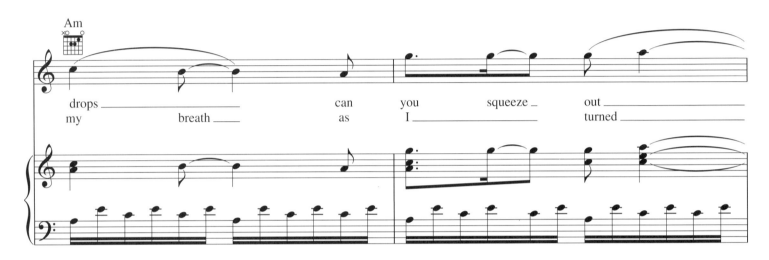

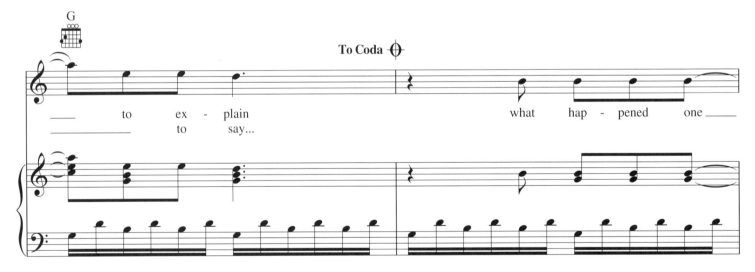

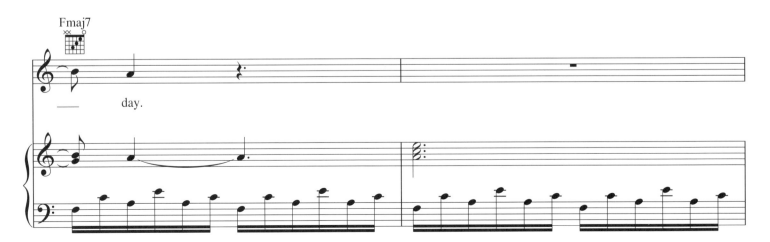

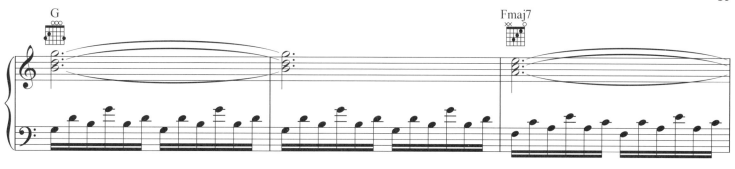

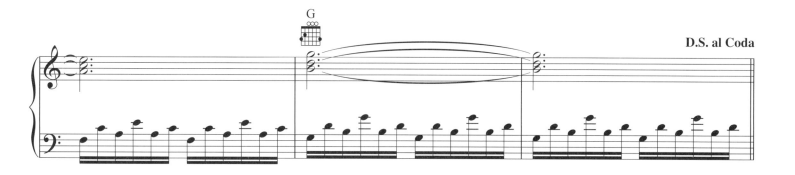

D.S. al Coda

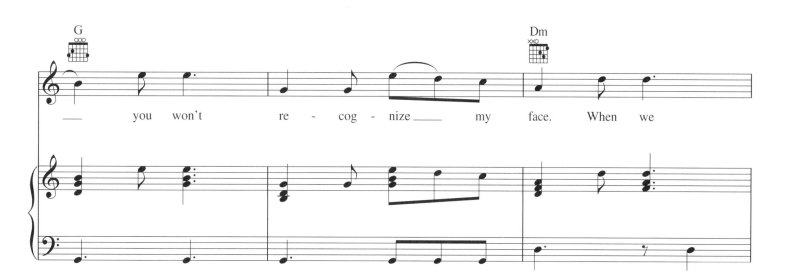

When we meet an - oth - er way, _____
up.

_____ you won't re - cog - nize _____ my face. When we

meet one way _____ or an-oth-er, you won't, you won't __ speak

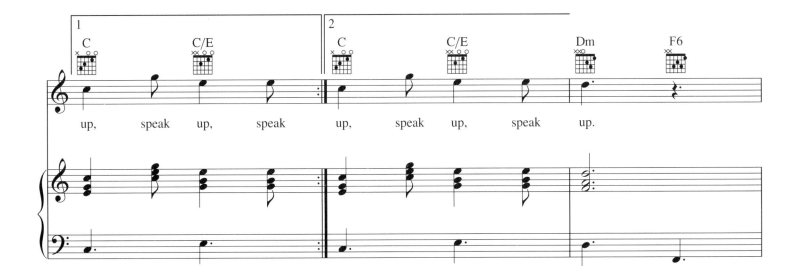

1 C ____ C/E ____ **2** C ____ C/E ____ Dm ____ F6

up, speak up, speak up, speak up, speak up.

Fmaj7 ____ G ____ Fmaj7

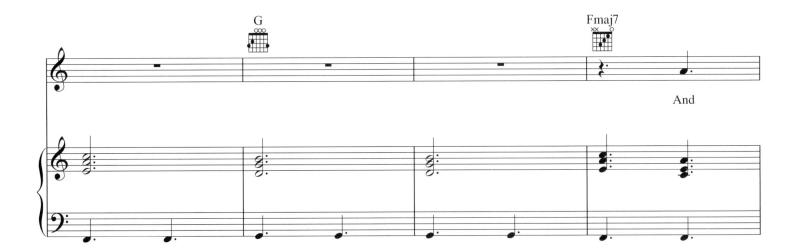

G ____ Fmaj7

And

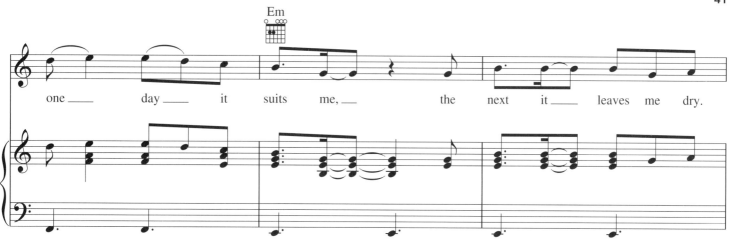

one __ day __ it suits me, __ the next it __ leaves me dry.

It plays __ out like a life - time, __ in

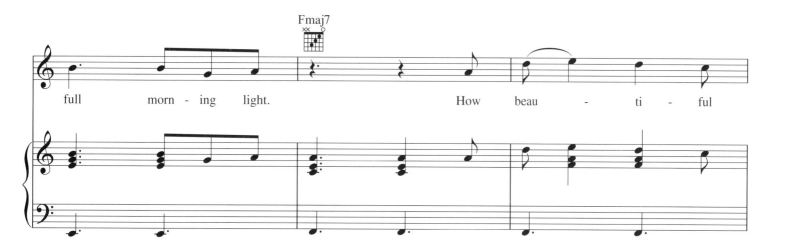

full morn - ing light. How beau - ti - ful

it was __ to be an - y - thing at all. But

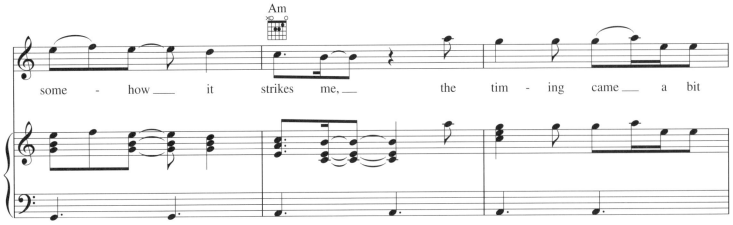

some - how ___ it strikes me, ___ the tim - ing came ___ a bit

off, oh. ___ When we meet an -
up.

oth - er way, ___ you won't re - cog - nize ___ my

face. When we meet one way ___ or an - oth - er, you

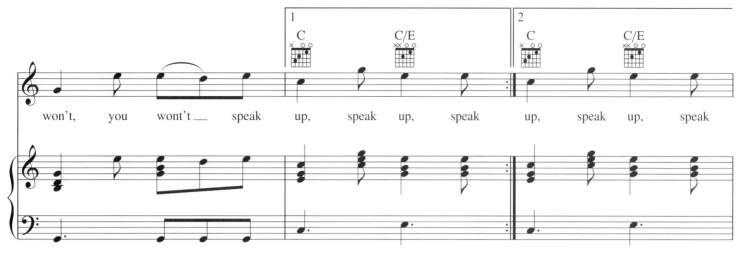

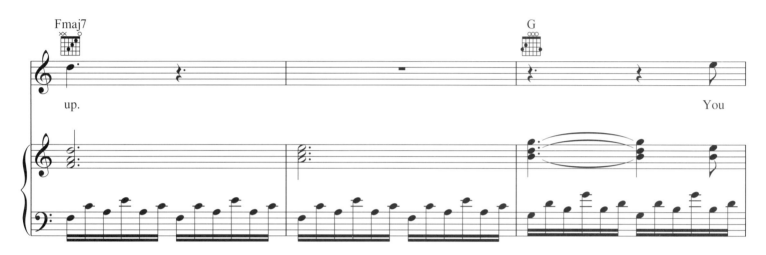

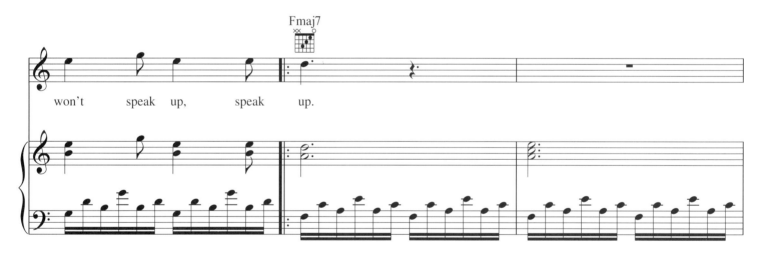

HEART OF STONE

Words and Music by KIERAN MARC SCRAGG
and NEIL REED

Moderate Piano Ballad

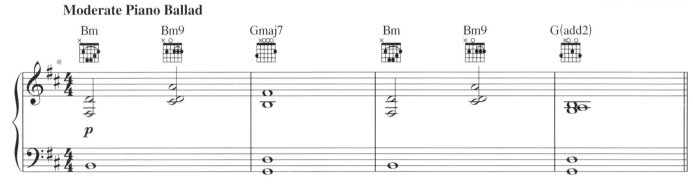

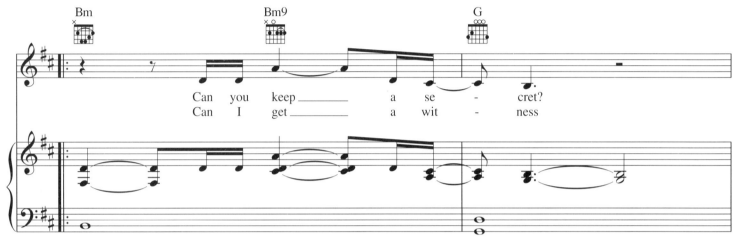

Can you keep _____ a se - cret?
Can I get _____ a wit - ness

Will it hold _____ your hand _____ a - mong the flames? _____
to the bruis - es and _____ the wast - ed tears? _____

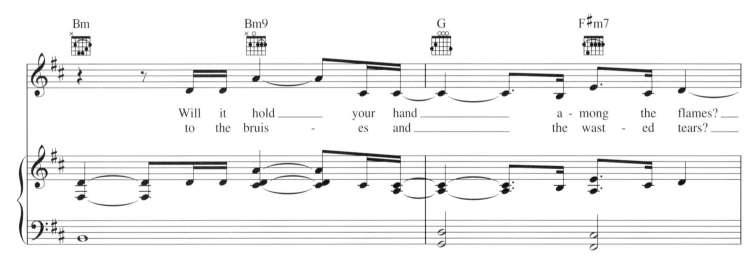

Hon - ey, you're _____ a ship - wreck _____ with your
You could dry _____ a riv - er _____ with your

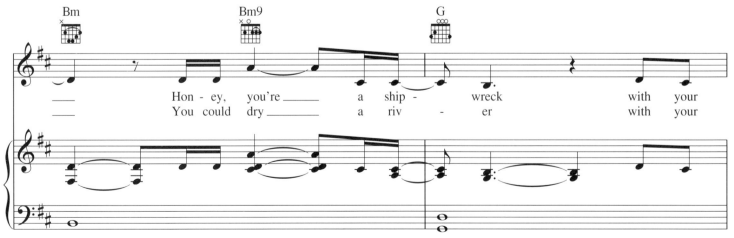

Recorded a half step lower.

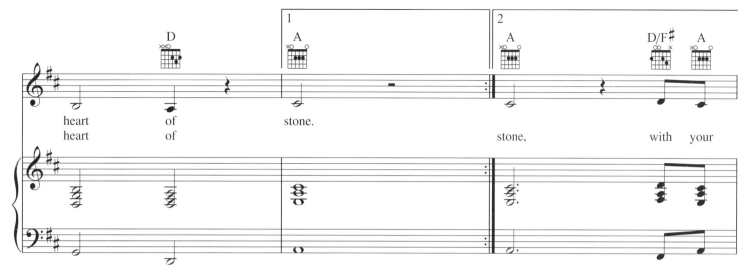

heart of stone.
heart of stone, with your

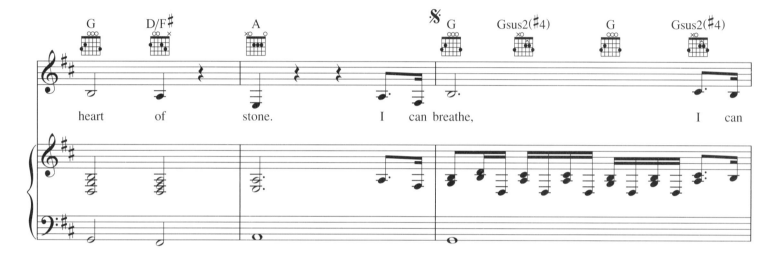

heart of stone. I can breathe, I can

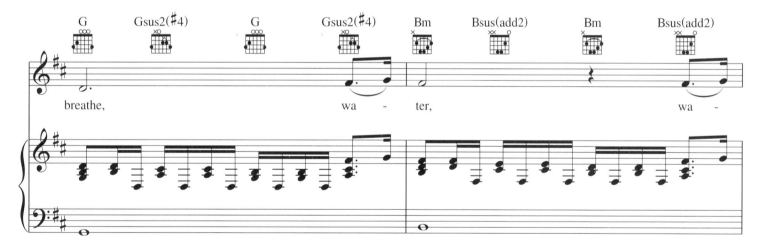

breathe, wa-ter, wa-

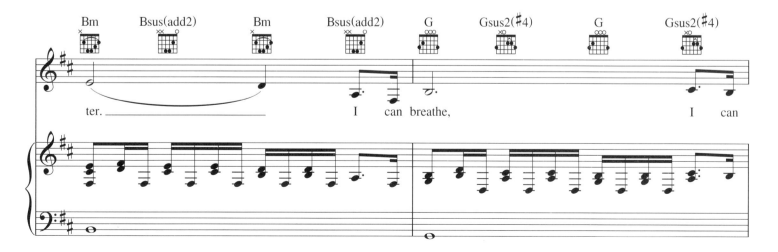

ter. I can breathe, I can

To Coda ⊕

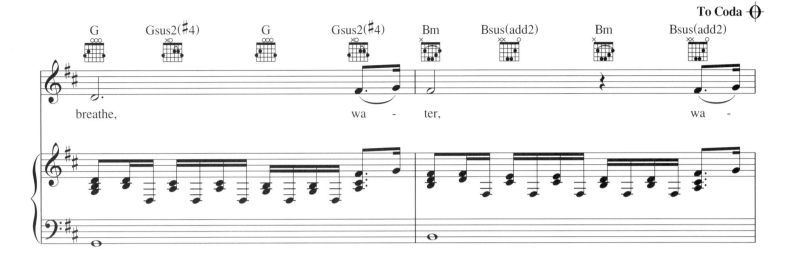

breathe, wa - ter, wa -

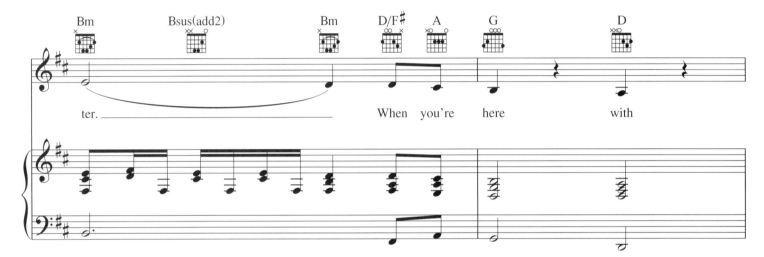

ter. _____ When you're here with

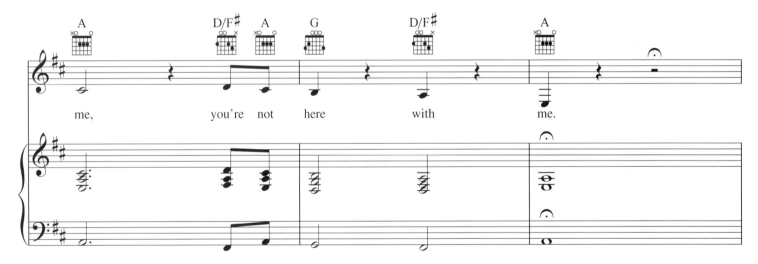

me, you're not here with me.

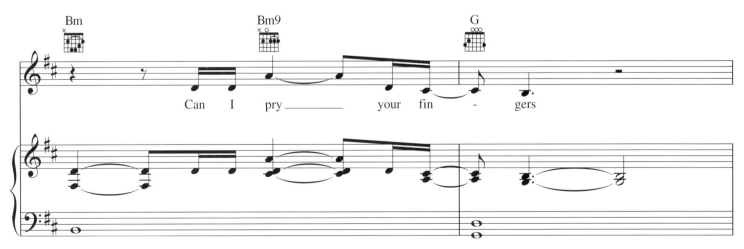

Can I pry _____ your fin - gers

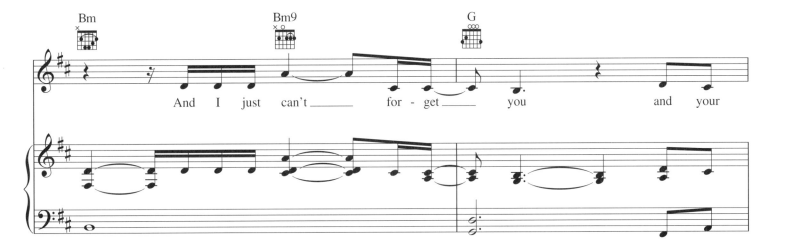

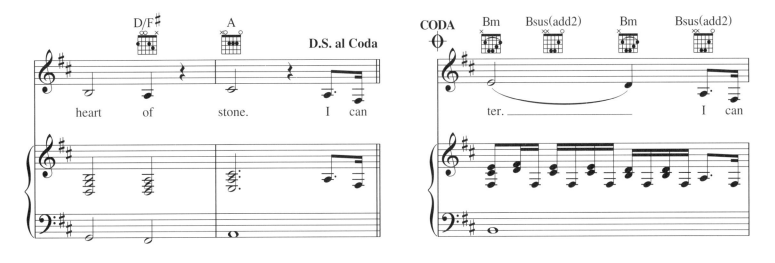

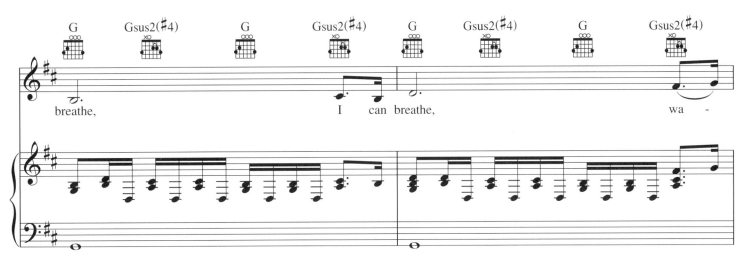

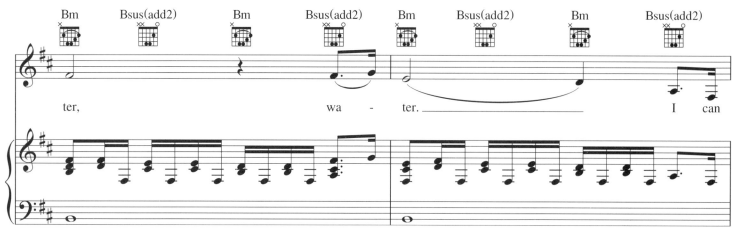

ter,   wa -   ter. _____ I can

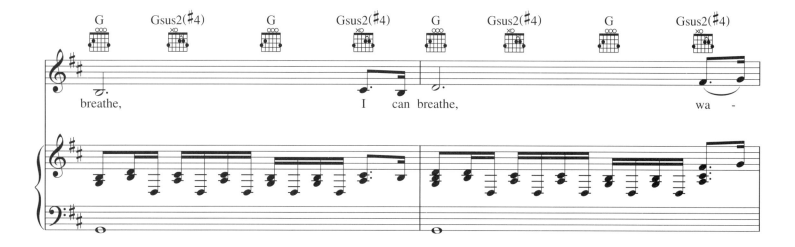

breathe,   I   can   breathe,   wa -

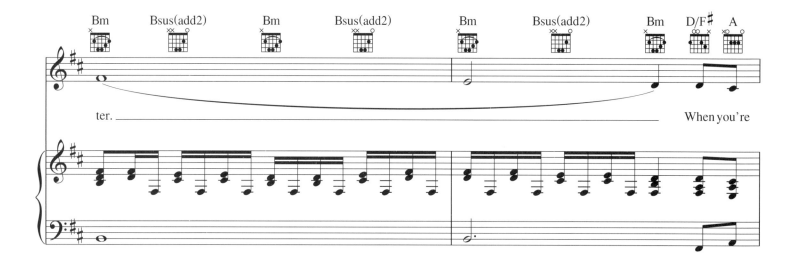

ter. _____ When you're

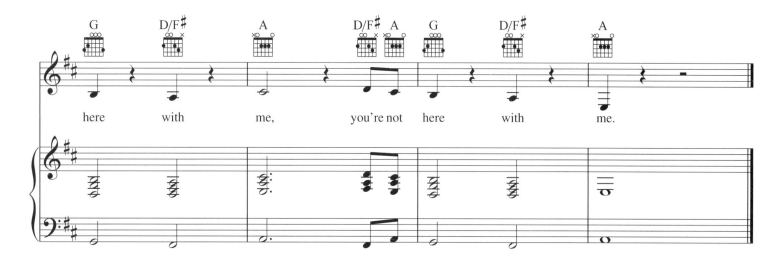

here   with   me,   you're not   here   with   me.

COVER YOUR TRACKS

Words and Music by
DAVID CAMERON WILTON

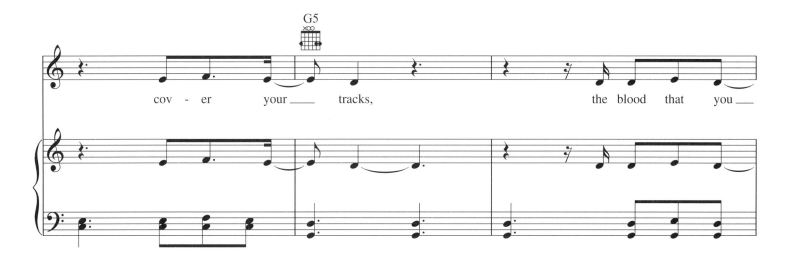

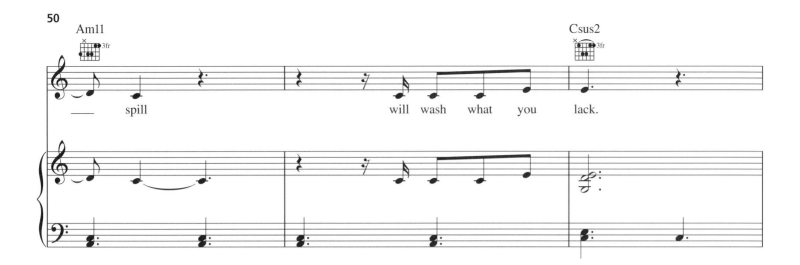

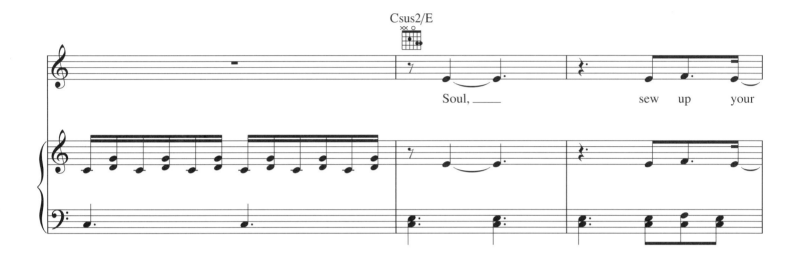

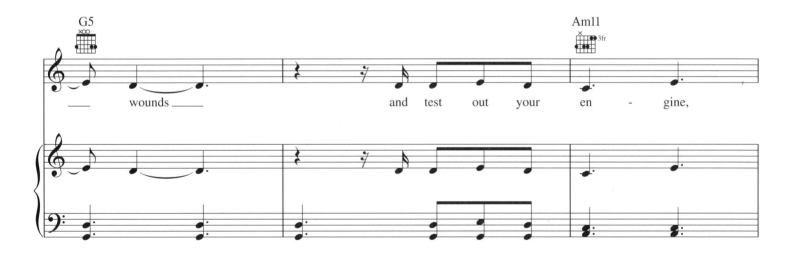

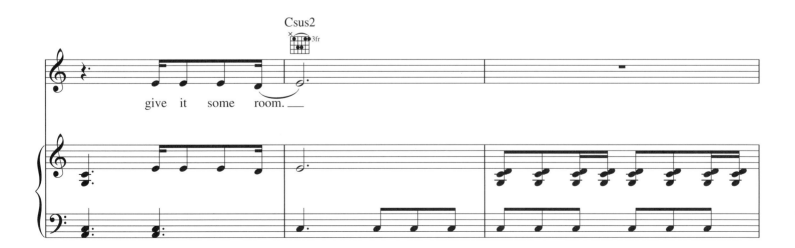

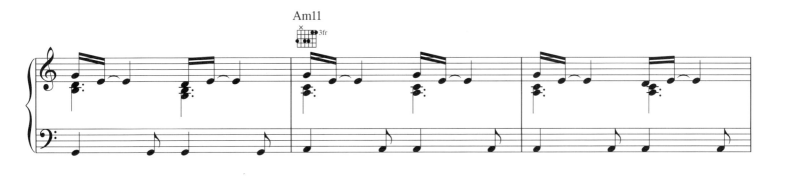

Life,

pick up your ___ pace, _____

cap - ture the

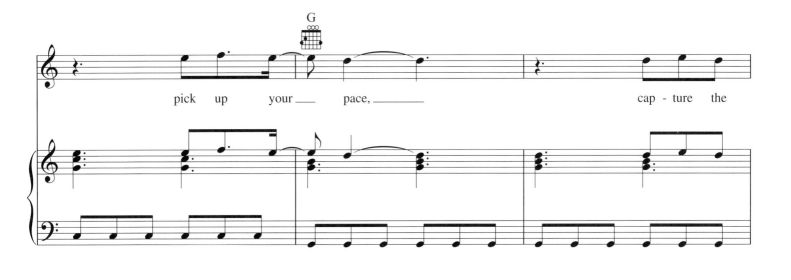

prize   you al - ways   chase. _____

_____   Soul,   o - pen your _____

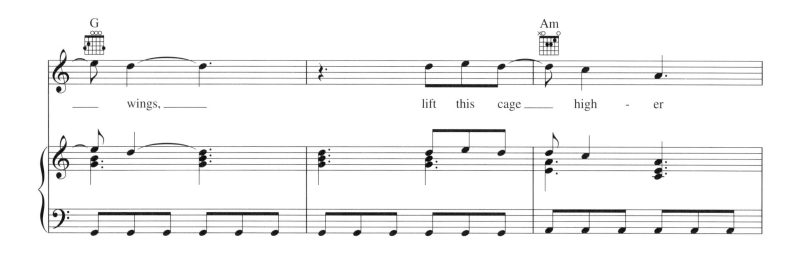

_____ wings, _____   lift this cage _____ high - er

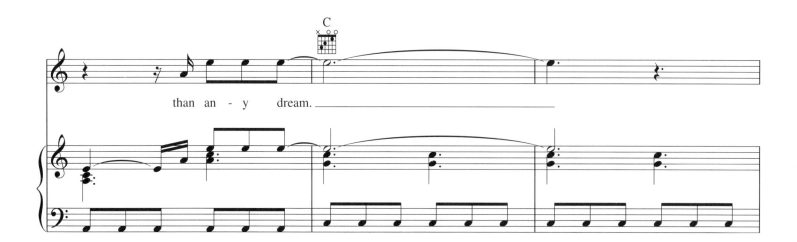

than an - y dream. _____

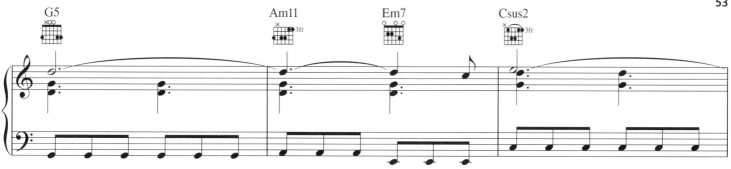

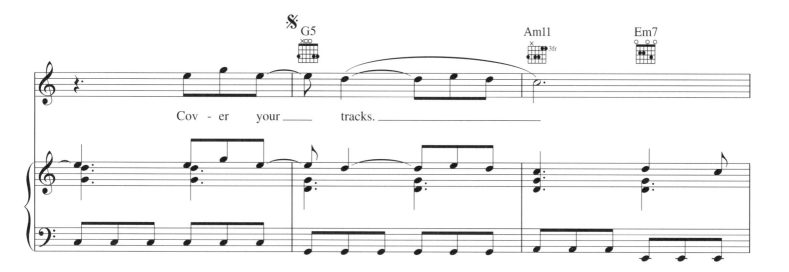

Cov - er your ____ tracks. _____

Sew up your ____ wounds. _____

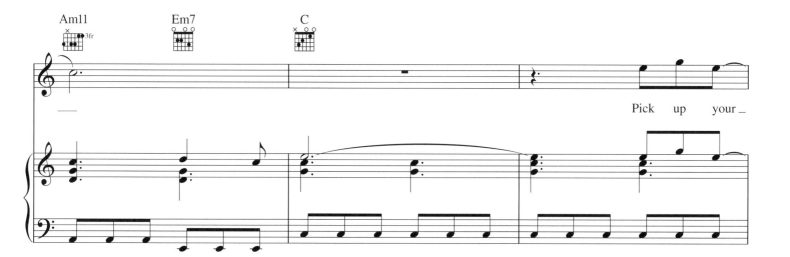

Pick up your __

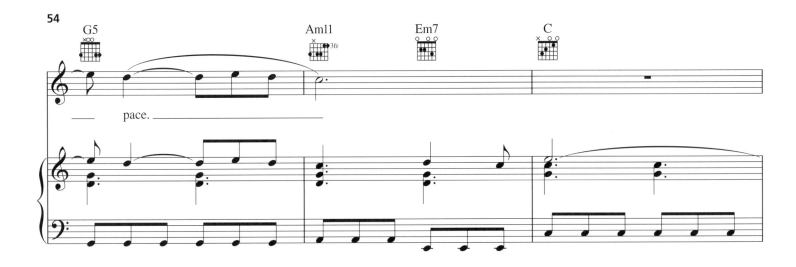

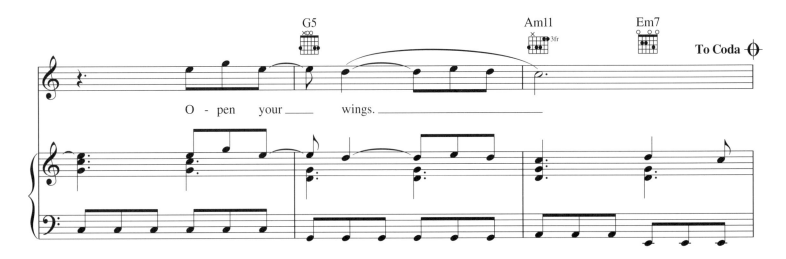

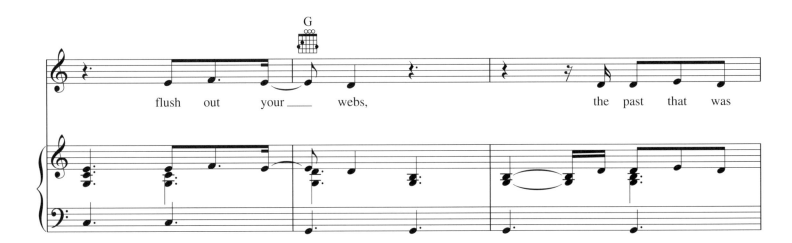

tan - gled will un - wrap and ___ shed. ___

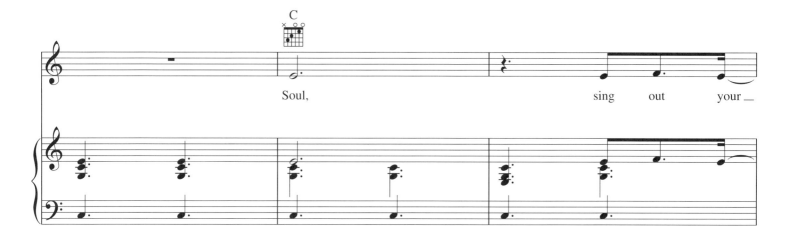

Soul, sing out your ___

___ songs, ___ clear out your ___ throat. ___

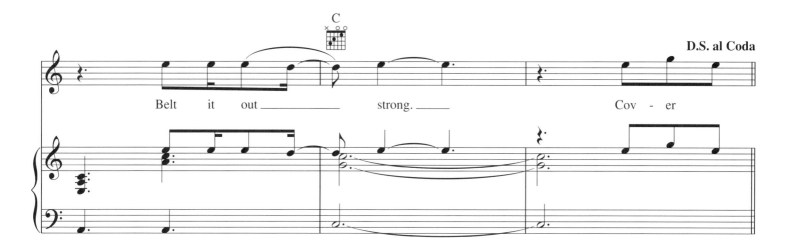

D.S. al Coda

Belt it out ___ strong. ___ Cov - er

CODA

Cov - er your ____ tracks. ____

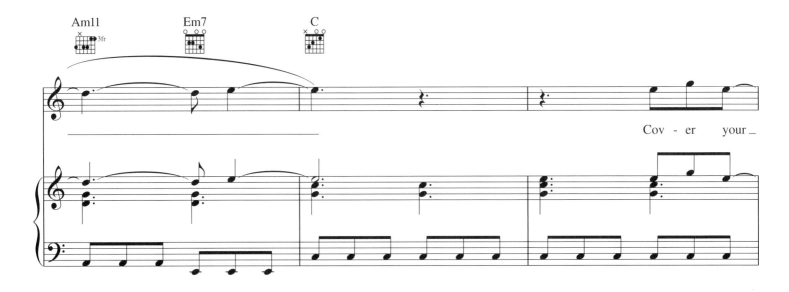

____ Cov - er your _

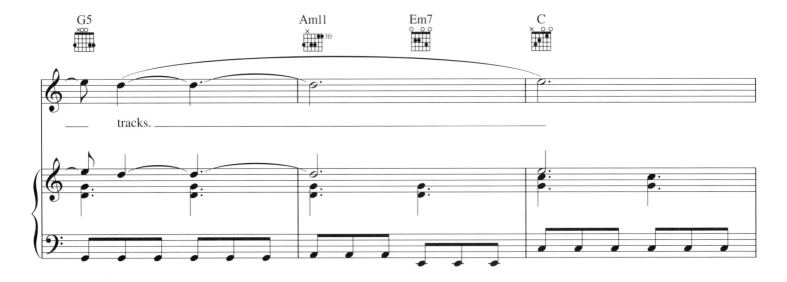

____ tracks. ____

GHOSTS
(We Are Ghosts)

Words and Music by
JAMES McMORROW

Moderately, subdued

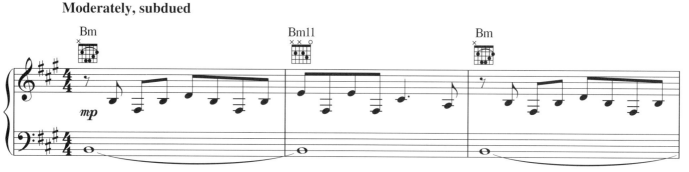

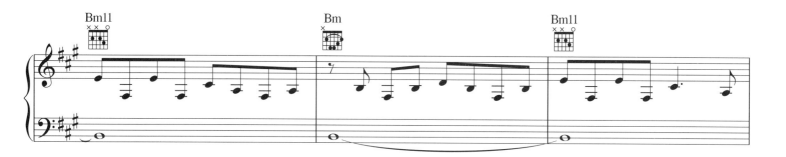

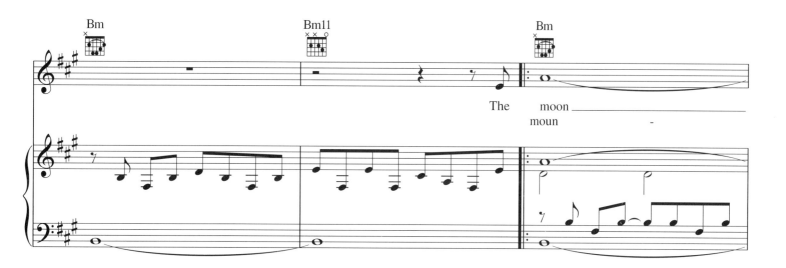

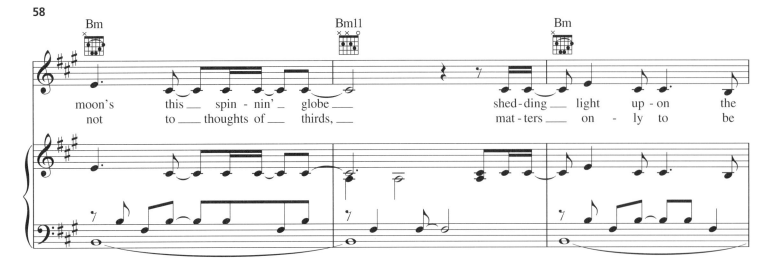

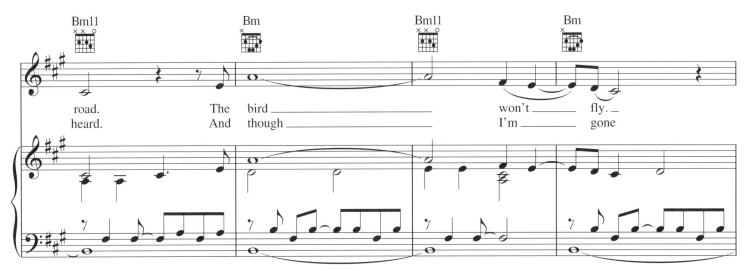

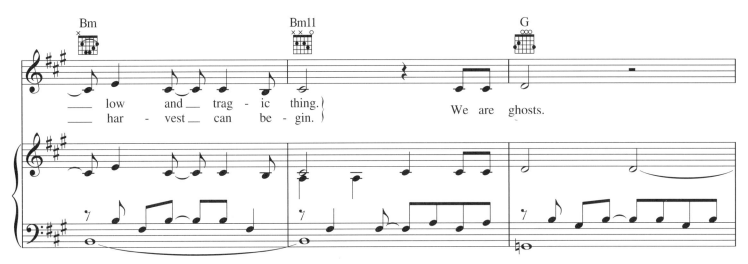

We are ghosts a-mongst these ___ hills. From the

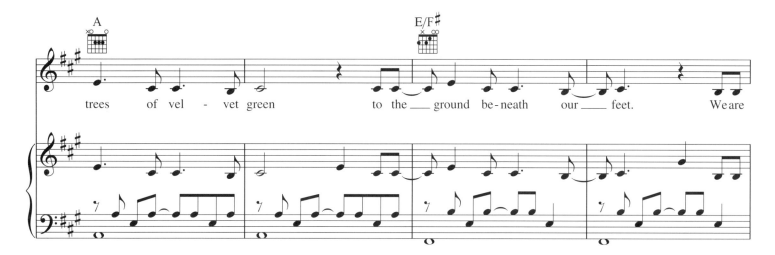

trees of vel - vet green to the ___ ground be-neath our ___ feet. We are

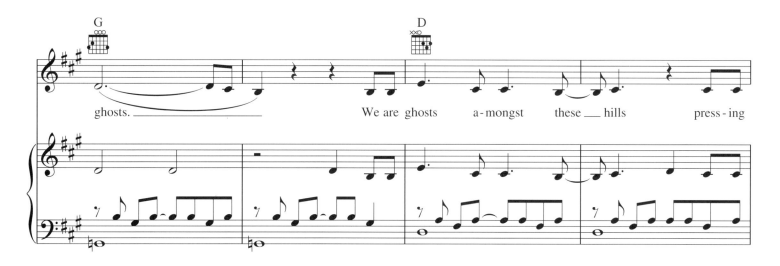

ghosts. _____ We are ghosts a-mongst these ___ hills press-ing

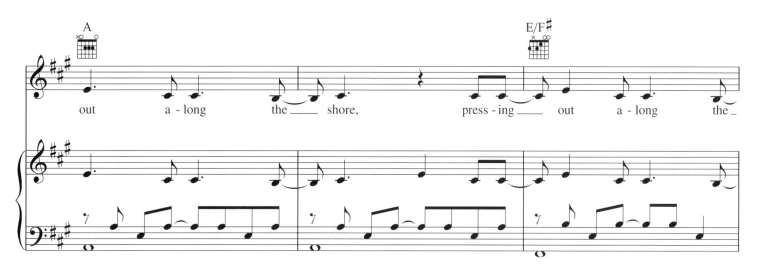

out a - long the ___ shore, press-ing ___ out a - long the ___

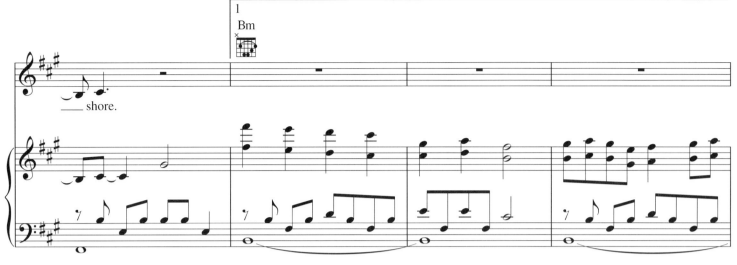

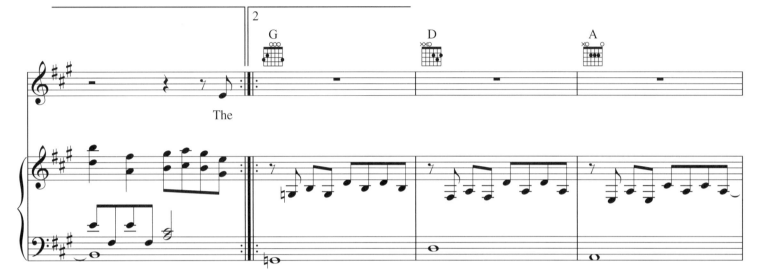

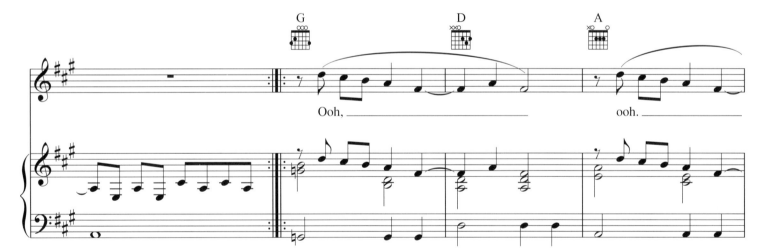

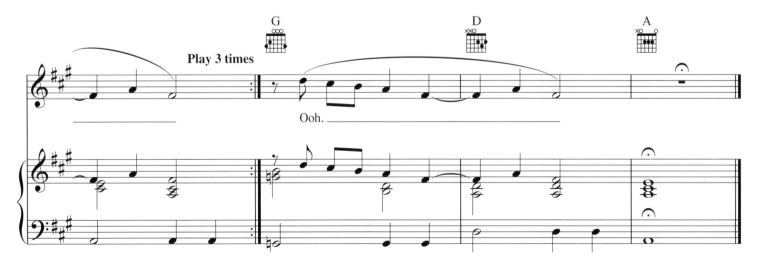

ALL I'VE EVER NEEDED

Words and Music by PAUL McDONALD
and NIKKI REED

Moderately slow ballad

* Male/Female duet (except where bindicated.)

62

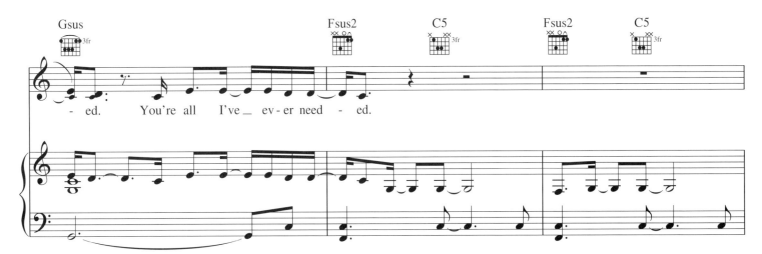

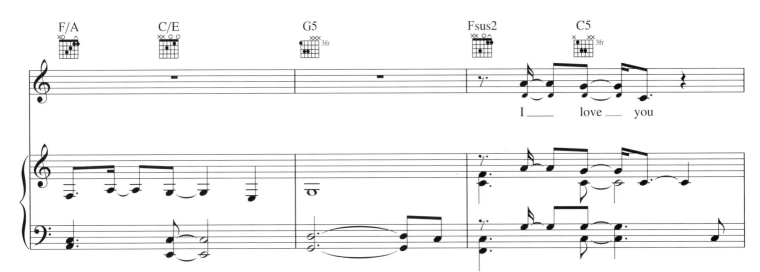

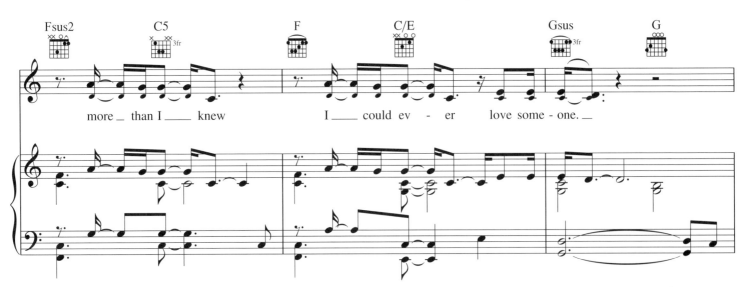

all, _____ ba - by you're all, _____ ba - by you're

all _____ I've __ ev - er need - ed. ____

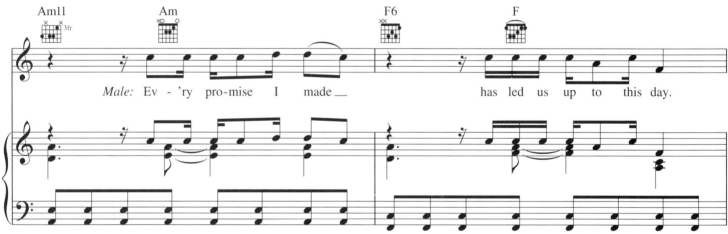

Male: Ev - 'ry pro - mise I made __ has led us up to this day.

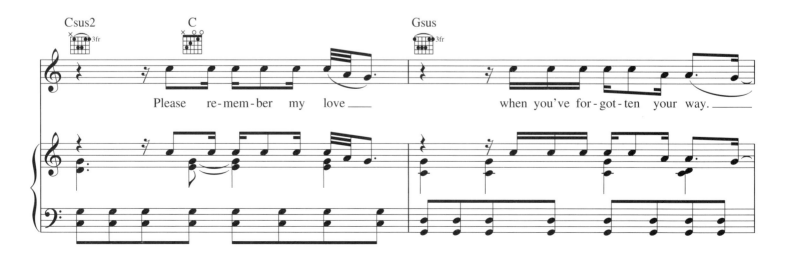

Please re - mem - ber my love __ when you've for - got - ten your way. ____

And this ache in my heart _____ makes me want to stand _ tall.

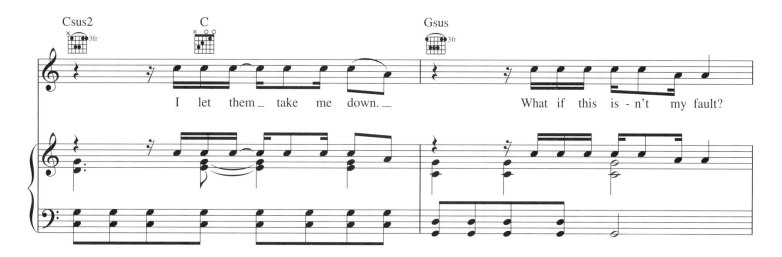

I let them _ take me down. _ What if this is-n't my fault?

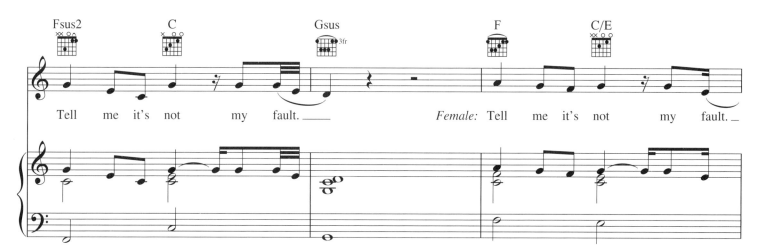

Tell me it's not my fault. _____ *Female:* Tell me it's not my fault. _

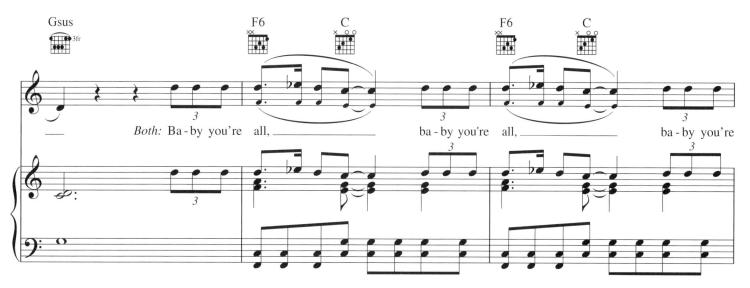

_ *Both:* Ba-by you're all, _____ ba-by you're all, _____ ba-by you're

all _____ I've __ ev-er need - ed. _____ Ba-by you're all, _____ ba-by you're

all, _____ ba - by you're all _____ I've __ ev - er need-

- ed. _____ You're all I've __ ev - er need - ed. _____

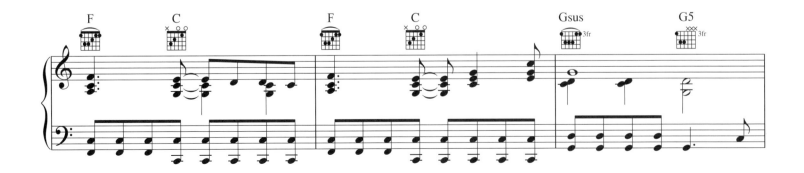

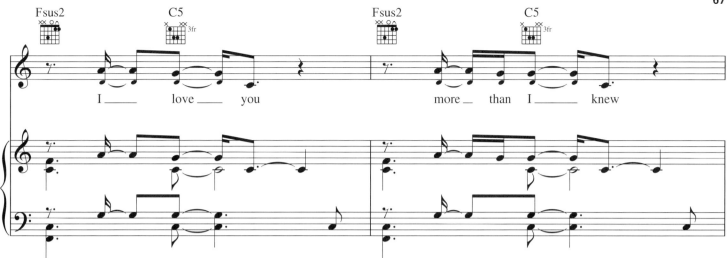

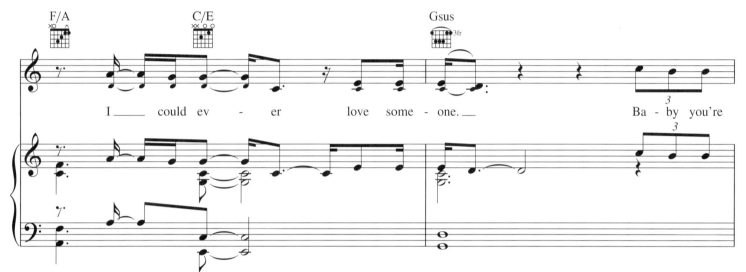

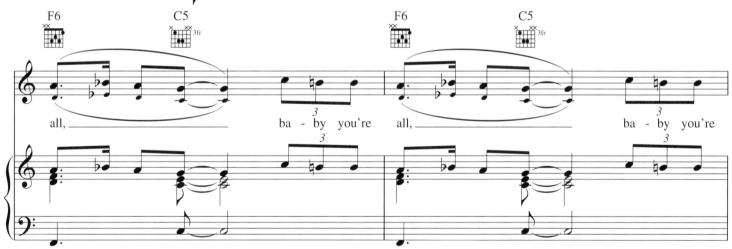

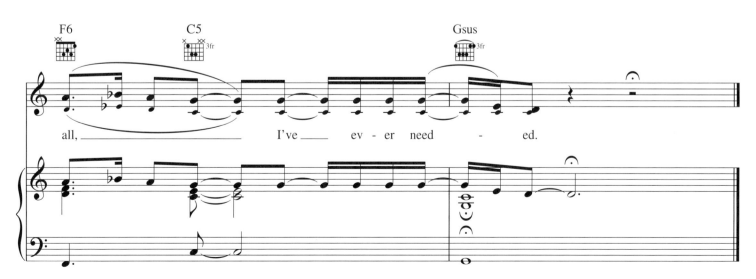

NEW FOR YOU

Words and Music by
REEVE CARNEY

Moody acoustic Ballad

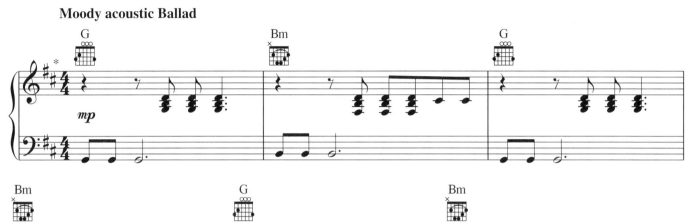

Ooh.

I can't for-get you, I ___ can't de-ny. ___

If I ___ sur-ren-der, ___ you hold ___ me and nev-

* Recorded a half-step lower

-er let go. ___ Your love's a mem - 'ry, mov - ing as one, _

___ my heart's a se - cret un - der your tongue. __ Cry - ing for - ev -

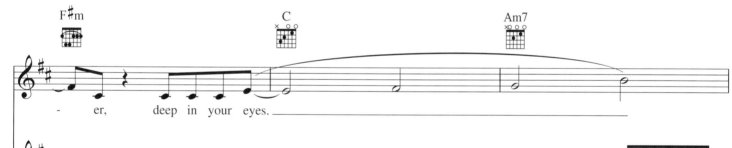

-er, deep in your eyes. ___

Al - ways, pic - tures of you and I, ___ they must

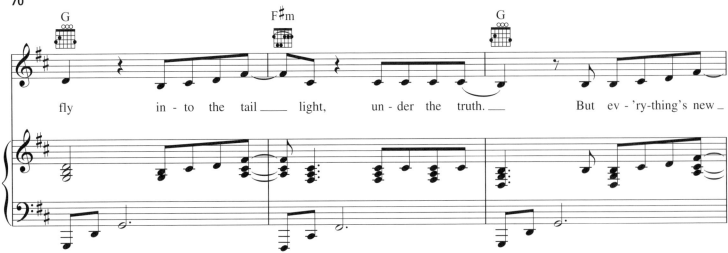

fly in - to the tail __ light, un - der the truth. __ But ev - 'ry-thing's new __

__ for you. And I would die a thous - and deaths

but to de - fend my __ hap - pi - ness, my love. __ Yours __ is like a

wave u - pon an o - pen __ shore, __ ev - 'ry time you fall, I on - ly want you more. __

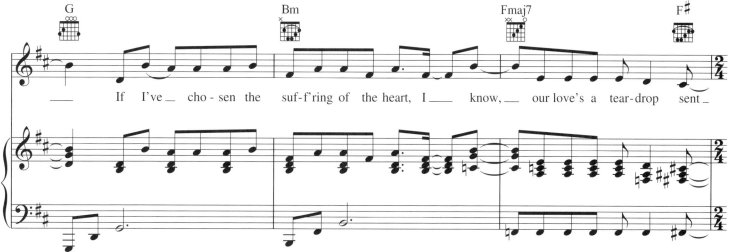

If I've __ cho-sen the suf-f'ring of the heart, I __ know, __ our love's a tear-drop sent __

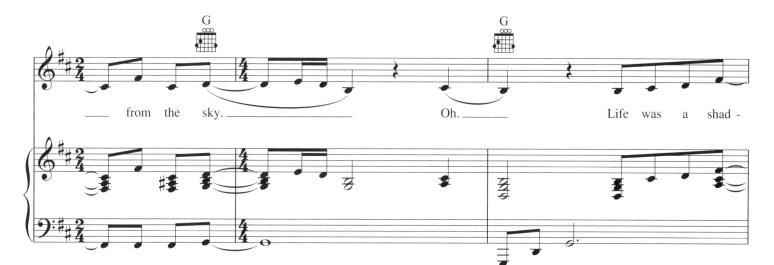

__ from the sky. __ Oh. __ Life was a shad-

-ow un-til I knew __ the sor-row's a si-lent cry-ing for you. __

__ I stand de-fense - less, deep in your eyes. __

Some - where, __ here in your love, __ I'm a - live. __

__ with you, ev - 'ry-thing chang - es, ev - 'ry-thing's new. __

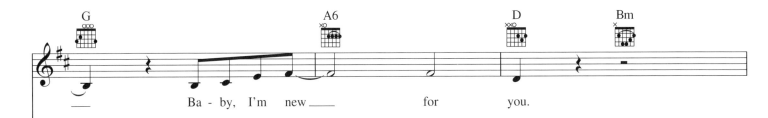

__ Ba - by, I'm new __ for you.

La da. Love's al - ways __ some-where be - hind __ you.

A THOUSAND YEARS
(Part 2)

Words and Music by DAVID HODGES
and CHRISTINA PERRI

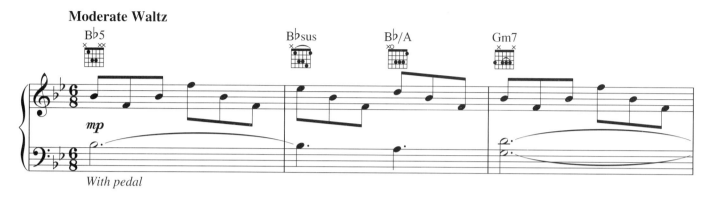

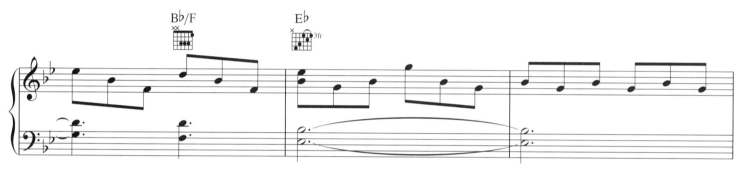

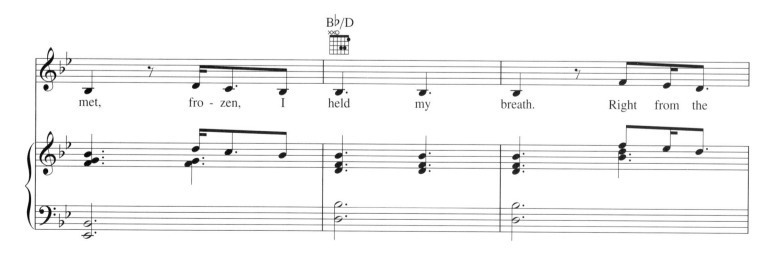

start I knew that I'd found a home. For my heart. Heart beats

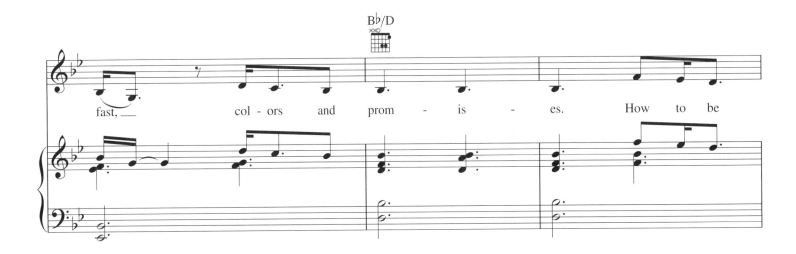

fast, ___ col - ors and prom - is - es. How to be

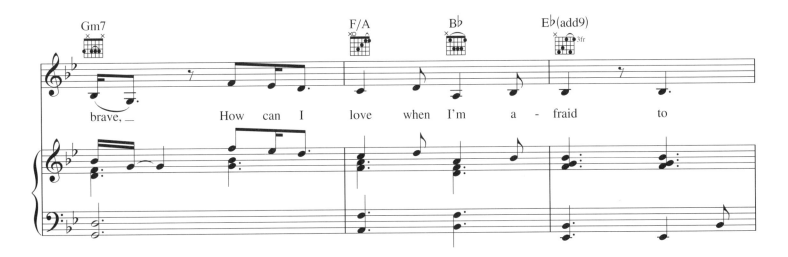

brave, ___ How can I love when I'm a - fraid to

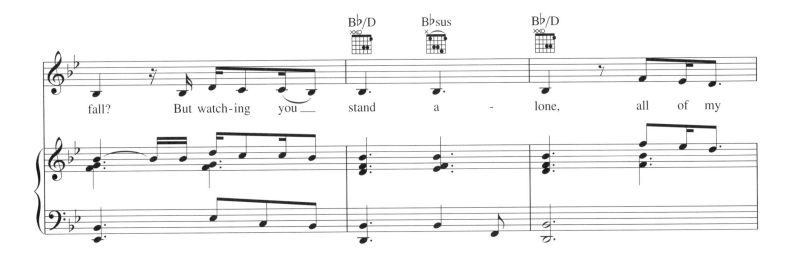

fall? But watch - ing you ___ stand a - lone, all of my

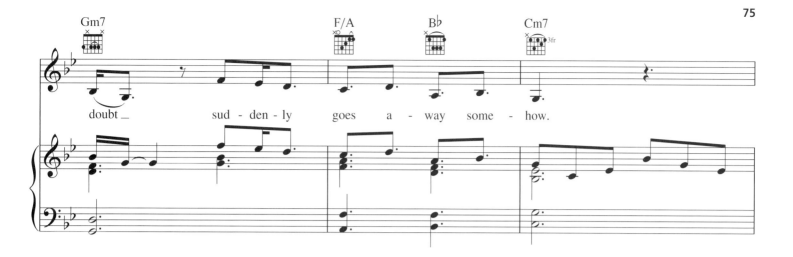

doubt __ sud - den - ly goes a - way some - how.

One step clos - er.

I have died ev - 'ry day wait - ing for __ you. Dar - ling don't be a - fraid,

I __ have loved __ you for a thou - sand years. __ I'll love you for a

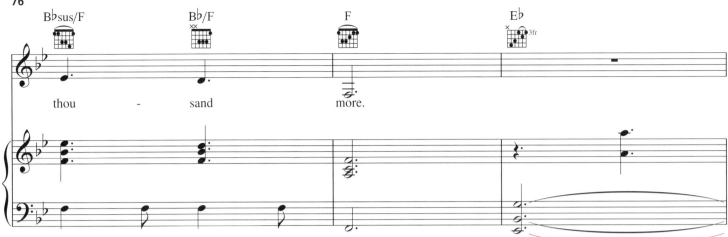

thou - sand more.

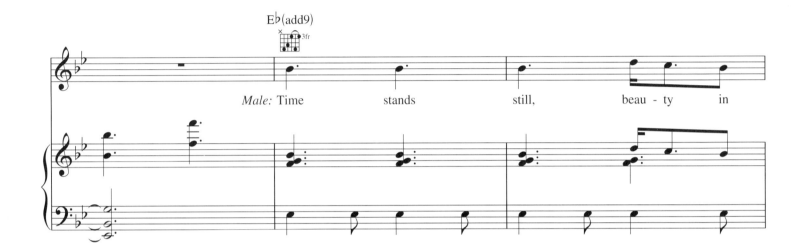

Male: Time stands still, beau - ty in

all she is. I will be brave. I will not

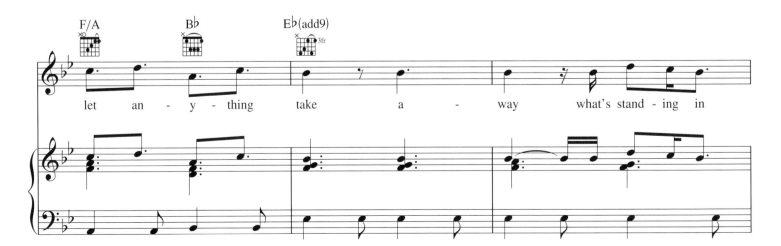

let an - y - thing take a - way what's stand - ing in

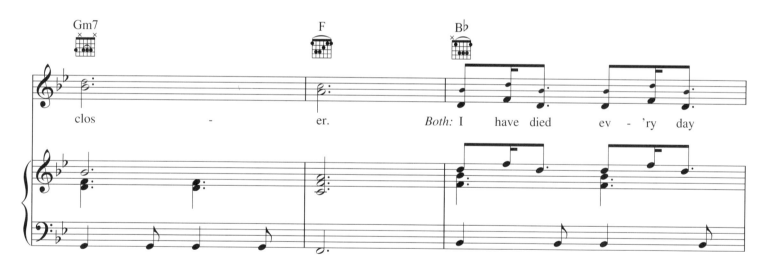

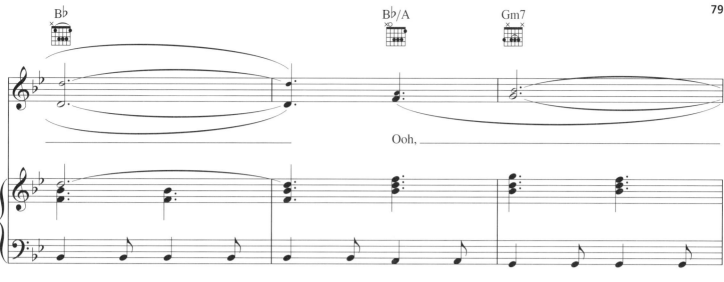

Ooh,

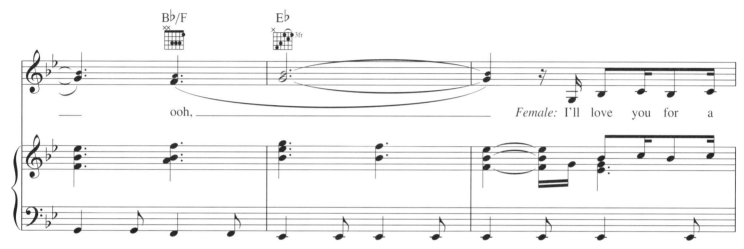

ooh, _____ *Female:* I'll love you for a

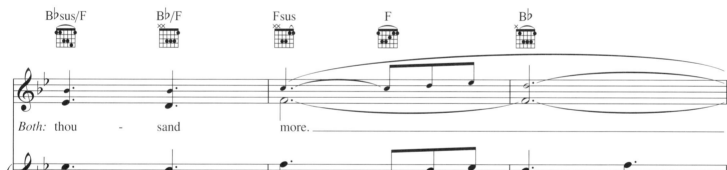

Both: thou - sand more. _____

Ooh,

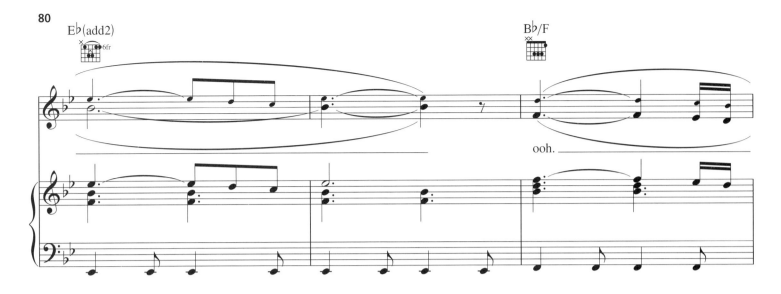

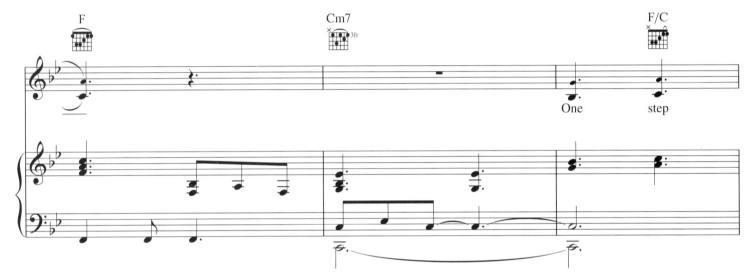

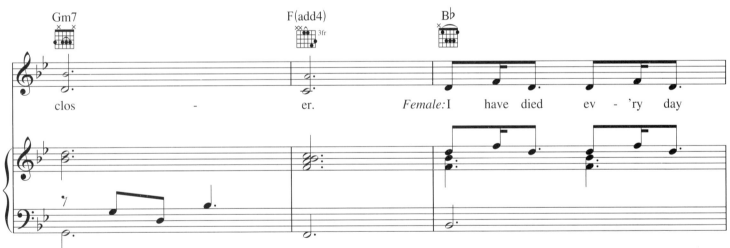

thou - sand years.___ I'll love you for a thou - sand

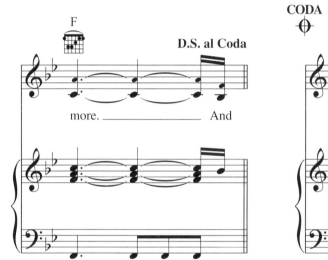

more.___ And

more.

PLUS QUE MA PROPRE VIE

Composed by
CARTER BURWELL

Flowing, with some freedom

poco a poco crescendo

ff

A little faster, with movement

mp

f

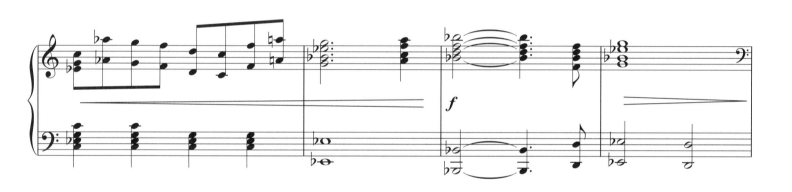

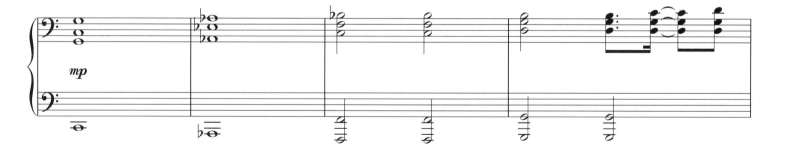

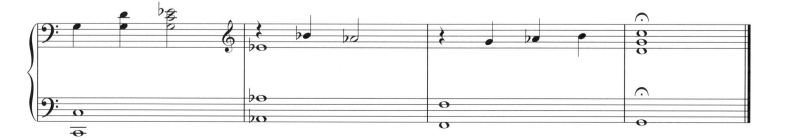